Reach the Highest Standard
in Professional Learning: Data

T0349513

Volumes in the Reach the Highest Standard in Professional Learning Series

Learning Communities

Leadership

Resources

Data

Learning Designs

Implementation

Outcomes

Reach the Highest Standard
in Professional Learning: Data

Thomas R. Guskey
Patricia Roy
Valerie von Frank

A Joint Publication

CORWIN
A SAGE Company

FOR INFORMATION:

Corwin

A SAGE Company

2455 Teller Road

Thousand Oaks, California 91320

(800) 233-9936

www.corwin.com

SAGE Publications Ltd.

1 Oliver's Yard

55 City Road

London EC1Y 1SP

United Kingdom

SAGE Publications India Pvt. Ltd.

B 1/I 1 Mohan Cooperative Industrial Area

Mathura Road, New Delhi 110 044

India

SAGE Publications Asia-Pacific Pte. Ltd.

3 Church Street

#10-04 Samsung Hub

Singapore 049483

Printed in the United States of America.

A catalog record of this book is available from the Library of Congress.

ISBN 978-1-4522-9177-2

This book is printed on acid-free paper.

Acquisitions Editor: Dan Alpert

Associate Editor: Kimberly Greenberg

Editorial Assistant: Cesar Reyes

Production Editor: Cassandra Margaret Seibel

Copy Editor: Terri Lee Paulsen

Typesetter: C&M Digitals (P) Ltd.

Proofreader: Rae-Ann Goodwin

Indexer: Jean Casalegno

Cover Designer: Gail Buschman

14 15 16 17 18 10 9 8 7 6 5 4 3 2 1

Contents

Introduction to the Series   vii
  Stephanie Hirsh

**The Learning Forward Standards
for Professional Learning**   xi

The Data Standard   xiii

About the Authors   xvii

1. Using Data in Deliberate and Thoughtful Ways   1
  Thomas R. Guskey
  What Are Data?   2
  Multiple Sources of Data   3
  Begin With the Goals   6
  The Importance of Transparency in Gathering Data   8
  Types of Data   9
  Types of Student Learning Goals and Data   12
  Relationships Among Types of Goals and Data   14
  Levels of Data   15
  Attainment Versus Improvement Student Data   21
  Evaluating Professional Learning   23
  The Importance of Backward Planning   35
  Summary   37
  References   37

**2. Using Data to Make Professional
Learning Decisions**   44
  Patricia Roy
  Analyze Student, Educator, and System Data   50
  Assessing Progress   57

Evaluate Professional Learning   65
Conclusion   74
References   76

3. The Case Study   **78**
Valerie von Frank
A New Beginning   80
Clear Expectations for Student Achievement   82
Aligning the Curriculum, Assessments, Standards   83
Monitoring Throughout the System   84
Support for Student Learning   85
Teacher Evaluation and Recruitment   88
A Culture of Data-Driven Decisions   89
Long-Term Commitment   92
Case Study Discussion Questions   96
Reference   97

Index   **98**

Introduction to the Series

These are the demands on educators and school systems right now, among many others:

- They must fulfill the moral imperative of educating every child for tomorrow's world, regardless of background or status.
- They must be prepared to implement college- and career-ready standards and related assessments.
- They must implement educator evaluations tied to accountability systems.

A critical element in creating school systems that can meet these demands is building the capacity of the system's educators at all levels, from the classroom teacher to the instructional coach to the school principal to the central office administrator, and including those partners who work within and beyond districts. Building educator capacity in this context requires effective professional learning.

Learning Forward's Standards for Professional Learning define the essential elements of and conditions for professional learning that leads to changed educator practices and improved student results. They are grounded in the understanding that the ultimate purpose of professional learning is increasing student success. Educator effectiveness—and this includes all educators working in and with school systems, not just teachers—is linked closely to student learning. Therefore increasing the effectiveness of educators is a key lever to school improvement.

Effective professional learning happens in a culture of continuous improvement, informed by data about student and educator performance and supported by leadership and sufficient resources.

Educators learning daily have access to information about relevant instructional strategies and resources and, just as important, time for collaboration with colleagues, coaches, and school leaders. Education leaders and systems that value effective professional learning provide not only sufficient time and money but also create structures that reinforce monitoring and evaluation of that learning so they understand what is effective and have information to adjust and improve.

WHY STANDARDS?

Given that any system can—and must—develop expertise about professional learning, why are standards important? Among many reasons are these:

First, adherence to standards ensures equity. When learning leaders across schools and systems agree to follow a common set of guidelines, they are committing to equal opportunities for all the learners in those systems. If all learning is in alignment with the Standards for Professional Learning and tied to student and school improvement goals, then all educators have access to the best expertise available to improve their practice and monitor results.

Standards also provide a common language that allows for conversation, collaboration, and implementation planning that crosses state, regional, and national borders. This collaboration can leverage expertise from any corner of the world to change practice and results.

Finally, standards offer guidelines for accountability. While an endorsement of the standards doesn't in itself guarantee quality, they provide a framework within which systems can establish measures to monitor progress, alignment, and results.

FROM STANDARDS TO TRANSFORMATION

So a commitment to standards is a first critical step. Moving into deep understanding and sustained implementation of standards is another matter. Transforming practices, and indeed, whole systems, will require long-term study, planning, and evaluation.

Reach the Highest Standard in Professional Learning is created to be an essential set of tools to help school and system leaders take those steps. As with the Standards for Professional Learning themselves, there will be seven volumes, one for each standard.

While the standards were created to work in synergy, we know that educators approach professional learning from a wide range of experiences, concerns, expertise, and passions. Perhaps a school leader may have started PLCs in his school to address a particular learning challenge, and thus has an abiding interest in how learning communities can foster teacher quality and better results. Maybe a central office administrator started her journey to standards-based professional learning through a study of how data informs changes, and she wants to learn more about the foundations of data use. This series was created to support such educators and to help them continue on their journey of understanding systemwide improvement and the pieces that make such transformation possible.

In developing this series of books on the Standards for Professional Learning, Corwin and Learning Forward envisioned that practitioners would enter this world of information through one particular book, and that their needs and interests would take them to all seven as the books are developed. The intention is to serve the range of needs practitioners bring and to support a full understanding of the elements critical to effective professional learning.

All seven volumes in Reach the Highest Standard in Professional Learning share a common structure, with components to support knowledge development, exploration of changes in practice, and a vision of each concept at work in real-world settings.

In each volume, readers will find

- A think piece developed by a leading voice in the professional learning field. These thought leaders represent both scholars and practitioners, and their work invites readers to consider the foundations of each standard and to push understanding of those seven standards.
- An implementation piece that helps readers put the think piece and related ideas into practice, with tools for both individuals and groups to use in reflection and discussion about the standards. Shirley M. Hord and Patricia Roy, long-standing Learning Forward standards leaders, created the implementation pieces across the entire series.
- A case study that illuminates what it looks like in schools and districts when education leaders prioritize the standards in

their improvement priorities. Valerie von Frank, with many years of writing about education in general and professional learning in particular, reported these pieces, highlighting insights specific to each standard.

Moving Toward Transformation

We know this about effective professional learning: Building awareness isn't enough to change practice. It's a critical first piece, and these volumes will help in knowledge development. But sustaining knowledge and implementing change require more.

Our intention is that the content and structure of the volumes can move readers from awareness to changes in practice to transformation of systems. And of course transformation requires much more. Commitment to a vision for change is an exciting place to start. A long-term informed investment of time, energy, and resources is non-negotiable, as is leadership that transcends one visionary leader who will inevitably move on.

Ultimately, it will be the development of a culture of collective responsibility for all students that sustains improvement. We invite you to begin your journey toward developing that culture through study of the Standards for Professional Learning and through Reach the Highest Standard in Professional Learning. Learning Forward will continue to support the development of knowledge, tools, and evidence that inform practitioners and the field. Next year's challenges may be new ones, and educators working at their full potential will always be at the core of reaching our goals for students.

Stephanie Hirsh
Executive Director, Learning Forward

The Learning Forward Standards for Professional Learning

Learning Communities: Professional learning that increases educator effectiveness and results for all students occurs within learning communities committed to continuous improvement, collective responsibility, and goal alignment.

Leadership: Professional learning that increases educator effectiveness and results for all students requires skillful leaders who develop capacity, advocate, and create support systems for professional learning.

Resources: Professional learning that increases educator effectiveness and results for all students requires prioritizing, monitoring, and coordinating resources for educator learning.

Data: Professional learning that increases educator effectiveness and results for all students uses a variety of sources and types of student, educator, and system data to plan, assess, and evaluate professional learning.

Learning Designs: Professional learning that increases educator effectiveness and results for all students integrates theories, research, and models of human learning to achieve its intended outcomes.

Implementation: Professional learning that increases educator effectiveness and results for all students applies research on change and sustains support for implementation of professional learning for long-term change.

Outcomes: Professional learning that increases educator effectiveness and results for all students aligns its outcomes with educator performance and student curriculum standards.

Source: Learning Forward. (2011). *Standards for Professional Learning.* Oxford, OH: Author.

The Data Standard

Professional learning that increases educator effective-ness and results for all students uses a variety of sources and types of student, educator, and system data to plan, assess, and evaluate professional learning.

Data from multiple sources enrich decisions about professional learning that leads to increased results for every student. Multiple sources include both quantitative and qualitative data, such as common formative and summative assessments, performance assessments, observations, work samples, performance metrics, portfolios, and self-reports. The use of multiple sources of data offers a balanced and more comprehensive analysis of student, educator, and system performance than any single type or source of data can. However, data alone do little to inform decision making and increase effectiveness.

Thorough analysis and ongoing use are essential for data to inform decisions about professional learning, as is support in the effective analysis and use of data.

ANALYZE, STUDENT, EDUCATOR, AND SYSTEM DATA

Data about students, educators, and systems are useful in defining individual, team, school, and system goals for professional learning. Probing questions guide data analysis to understand where students are in relationship to the expected curriculum standards and to identify the focus for educator professional learning. Student data include formal and informal assessments, achievement data such as grades and annual, benchmark, end-of-course, and daily classroom work, and classroom assessments. Other forms of data, such as those that cover demographics, engagement, attendance, student perceptions, behavior and discipline, participation in extracurricular programs, and post-graduation education, are useful in understanding student learning needs, particularly if they are analyzed by student characteristics.

Knowing student learning needs guides decisions about educator professional learning, yet student data alone are insufficient. A comprehensive understanding of educator learning needs is essential to planning meaningful professional learning. Sample data to consider for identifying goals for educator learning include preparation information, performance on various assessments, educator perceptions, classroom or work performance, student results, and individual professional learning goals.

Changes at the student and educator levels are best sustained when school and system-level learning occur simultaneously. School and system administrators also engage in data collection and analysis to determine changes in policy, procedures, fiscal resources, human resources, time, or technology, for example, needed to support school- and team-based learning. Administrators might analyze data about inputs, such as fiscal, personnel, and time allocation; outputs, such as frequency of participation, level of engagement, and type of communication; and outcomes, such as changes in educator practice and student achievement.

ASSESS PROGRESS

Data also are useful to monitor and assess progress against established benchmarks. At the classroom level, teachers use student data to assess the effectiveness of the application of their new learning. When teachers, for example, design assessments and scoring guides and engage in collaborative analysis of student work, they gain crucial information about the effect of their learning on students. Evidence of ongoing increases in student learning is a powerful motivator for teachers during the inevitable setbacks that accompany complex change efforts.

At the school level, leadership teams use data to monitor implementation of professional learning and its effects on educator practice and student learning. Engaging teams of teacher leaders and administrators in analyzing and interpreting data, for example, provides them a more holistic view of the complexity of school improvement and fosters collective responsibility and accountability for student results.

Frequent collection and use of data about inputs, outputs, and outcomes of professional learning reinforce the cycle of continuous improvement by allowing for ongoing adjustments in the learning process to increase results for students, educators, and systems. Ongoing data collection, analysis, and use, especially when done in teams, provide stakeholders with information that sustains momentum and informs continuous improvement.

EVALUATE PROFESSIONAL LEARNING

Those responsible for professional learning implement and maintain standards for professional learning and use the standards to monitor, assess, and evaluate it. Well-designed evaluation of professional learning provides information needed to increase its quality and effectiveness. Evaluation of professional learning also provides useful information for those who advocate for professional learning; those responsible for engaging in, planning, facilitating, or supporting professional learning; and those who want to know about the contribution of professional learning to student achievement.

Internal and external evaluators conduct evaluations of professional learning. Some professional learning, such as programs funded through grants or other special funding, requires formal, external evaluations. Whether or not an external evaluation is required, all professional learning should be evaluated on an ongoing basis for its effectiveness and results. For example, a school system might engage in a rigorous evaluation of its mentoring and induction program every three years and collect other output data annually for formative assessment.

Questions that guide the evaluation of professional learning address its worth, merit, and effects. Evaluation questions are designed based on the goals of professional learning and the various audiences interested in the evaluation. For example, federal policy makers might want to know if the investment in professional learning contributed to changes in student achievement. School system leaders may want to know if increasing time for teacher collaboration and adding coaches result in changes in teacher practice and student learning. Teachers might want to know if the implementation of new instructional practices increased their effectiveness with certain types of students. Evaluators design a process to answer the evaluation questions, gather quantitative and qualitative data from various sources, analyze and interpret the data, form conclusions, and recommend future actions.

Evaluation of professional learning includes examination of data related to inputs, outputs, and outcomes. Evaluation of professional learning follows a rigorous process, international standards for evaluation, and a code of ethics for evaluators.

Source: Learning Forward. (2011). *Standards for Professional Learning.* Oxford, OH: Author.

About the Authors

Dr. Thomas R. Guskey is Professor of Educational Psychology in the College of Education at the University of Kentucky. A graduate of the University of Chicago, he began his career in education as a middle school teacher, served as an administrator in Chicago Public Schools, and was the first director of the Center for the Improvement of Teaching and Learning, a national educational research center. He is the author/editor of 20 books and over 200 articles published in prominent research journals as well as *Educational Leadership, Kappan,* and *School Administrator.* Dr. Guskey served on the Policy Research Team of the National Commission on Teaching and America's Future, on the task force to develop the National Standards for Staff Development, and was named a fellow in the American Educational Research Association, which also honored him in 2006 for his outstanding contribution relating research to practice. His most recent books include *Answers to Essential Questions About Standards, Assessments, Grading, and Reporting* (with L. Jung, 2013), *Benjamin S. Bloom: Portraits of an Educator* (Ed.) (2012), *Developing Standards-Based Report Cards* (with J. Bailey, 2010), *Practical Solutions for Serious Problems in Standards-Based Grading* (Ed.) (2009), *The Principal as Assessment Leader* (Ed.) (2009), and *The Teacher as Assessment Leader* (Ed.) (2009).

 **Dr. Patricia Roy** is a senior consultant with Learning Forward's Center for Results. She works with state departments of education, districts, and schools across the United States as well as internationally. Most recently, she developed briefings and a resource guide to help schools use results from the revised Standards Assessment Inventory (SAI2) to improve professional learning. She has authored many articles and chapters on effective professional development, school improvement, innovation configuration maps, and cooperative learning. In her work with Learning Forward, Pat developed professional learning resource toolkits for Georgia; Arkansas; and Rochester, New York. She co-authored, with Joellen Killion, *Becoming a Learning School* and with Stephanie Hirsh, Joellen Killion, and Shirley Hord, *Standards Into Practice: Innovation Configurations for School-Based Roles* (2012). For five years, she wrote columns about implementing the Standards for Professional Development for *The Learning Principal* and *The Learning System,* two Learning Forward newsletters. She has also served as faculty for Professional Development Leadership Academy through the Arizona Department of Education. This 3-year program developed the knowledge and skills of school and district teams to plan, implement, and evaluate professional learning. She has also served as the founding director of the Delaware Professional Development Center in Dover, Deleware. The Center, developed by the Delaware State Education Association, focused on school improvement for student achievement and effective professional learning. She also served as the director of the Center for School Change in connection with a National Science Foundation SSI grant, a district coordinator of staff development, and an administrator in a regional educational consortium in Minnesota. Creating and improving professional learning so that it impacts student achievement is one of Pat's passions.

 **Valerie von Frank** is an author, editor, and communications consultant. A former newspaper editor and education reporter, she has focused much of her writing on education issues, including professional learning. She served as communications director in an urban school district and a nonprofit school reform organization and was the editor of *JSD,* the flagship magazine for the National Staff Development Council, now Learning Forward, for seven years. She has written extensively for education publications, including *JSD, Tools for Schools, The Learning System, The Learning Principal,* and *T3.* She is coauthor with Ann Delehant of *Making Meetings Work: How to Get Started, Get Going, and Get It Done* (Corwin, 2007); with Linda Munger of *Change, Lead, Succeed* (NSDC, 2010); with Robert Garmston of *Unlocking Group Potential to Improve Schools* (Corwin, 2012); and with Jennifer Abrams of *The Multigenerational Workplace: Communicate, Collaborate, and Create Community* (Corwin, 2014).

CHAPTER ONE

Using Data in Deliberate and Thoughtful Ways

Thomas R. Guskey

University of Kentucky

The *Standards for Professional Learning* are designed to guide educators in making thoughtful decisions about professional learning experiences that will increase "educator effectiveness and results for all students" (Learning Forward, 2011). Accomplishing this primary goal requires that those decisions be made based on relevant data. This requirement, in turn, makes the Data Standard an essential foundation for all of the other standards.

The Data Standard states: "Professional learning that increases educator effectiveness and results for all students uses a variety of sources and types of student, educator, and system data to plan, assess, and evaluate professional learning" (Learning Forward, 2011). Because of its indispensable and fundamental nature, no other standard is more important or more vital to the purpose of the *Standards for Professional Learning.*

In this chapter we will explore the meaning of "data" in the context of professional learning. We will consider the various types of data, the different purposes data can serve, and the many levels at which relevant data can be gathered and analyzed. Finally we turn to the use of data in evaluating professional learning endeavors and how to ensure those evaluations are meaningful and effective.

WHAT ARE DATA?

Data are defined as "factual information (as measurements or statistics) used as a basis for reasoning, discussion, or calculation" (see http://www.merriam-webster.com/dictionary/data). In other words, data are what we know. Some argue that data are not always factual and can be erroneous. Indeed, some of what we know or believe we know may be inaccurate. But in most cases those inaccuracies stem from the way the data were gathered (e.g., via biased or inadequate sampling) or the manner in which they were interpreted (e.g., through naïve, distorted, or prejudicial perspectives). Apart from these distortions, data represent facts.

By themselves, data are neither good nor bad; neither positive nor negative. Moreover, data have no meaning or intrinsic value when considered in isolation. They can be relevant or irrelevant, pertinent or immaterial. Data become meaningful and valuable *only* when processed, usually for the purpose of answering specific questions.

The usefulness of any particular set of data depends, therefore, on the context in which it is gathered, processed, and applied. For this reason, the key to successful data-based decision making rests not in the data, per se. Although data are essential to making apt decisions, the quality and appropriateness of particular data depend on their accuracy and relevance in answering specific questions in a particular context.

Because of the context-specific nature of data, discussion of data's appropriateness always must be preceded by the formulation of specific, essential questions. These questions provide the basis for all forms of inquiry, be it exploration, description, research, or evaluation. They guide selection of the most appropriate and meaningful data needed to answer the questions. They also determine the level of data needed, the type of analysis required, and the best means of reporting analysis results.

The most important first step in data-based decision making, therefore, is not a discussion of the data and how it will be analyzed or "mined." Rather, it is a discussion of the most important and essential questions that need to be addressed. Only when these questions are clearly articulated and agreed upon can meaningful discussions take place about what evidence, information, or data will be the most appropriate for answering those questions. After deciding what data are most appropriate, other issues regarding data collection and analysis become easier to address. Decisions about how to interpret the analysis, formulate conclusions, and derive implications for policy and practice become easier as well.

MULTIPLE SOURCES OF DATA

There are an infinite number of sources of data. In most modern education reforms, however, and particularly those guided by the requirements of the No Child Left Behind (NCLB) legislation (U.S. Congress, 2001), the primary data of interest are evidence on student learning derived from the results of large-scale assessments. Policy makers and legislators at the national, state, and provincial levels are attracted to large-scale assessment results as measures of reform success because they can be relatively inexpensive, relatively quick to implement, externally mandated, and the results are highly visible (Linn, 2000). These same policy makers and legislators also are convinced that good data on student performance drawn from large-scale assessments will help focus educators' attention and guarantee success, especially if consequences are attached to assessment results (see Elmore, 2004).

The large-scale assessment programs in most states and provinces are designed to measure students' "proficiency" on carefully articulated standards for student learning. The specific criteria that states and provinces use to define proficiency vary greatly in stringency and rigor, however, especially when compared to other assessment results, such as those from the National Assessment of Educational Progress (NAEP) in the United States (Linn, 2005; Peterson & Hess, 2005). These differences become more significant when the results from large-scale assessments are used to evaluate schools, students, or educators' professional learning for the purposes of accountability. Such initiatives affect numerous stakeholder groups, including school administrators, teachers, students, parents, school board members, future employers, and the community (Linn, 2003). But because the intent of most states' assessment and accountability programs is to monitor and improve the educational system, the stakes are highest for school administrators and teachers (Lane & Stone, 2002).

While the psychometric quality and validity of large-scale assessments for accountability purposes are widely debated (see Hill & DePascale, 2003; M. Kane, 2002), one point on which both advocates and critics agree is that they represent but one, potentially limited, indicator of student learning that might be considered in making decisions about schools, students, or professional learning. Significant evidence shows, for instance, that schools' results on large-scale assessments can be highly volatile (T. Kane & Staiger, 2002), and that relatively minor changes in design features for reporting results can lead to strikingly different categorizations of schools (Porter, Linn, & Trimble, 2005).

Concerns about these reliability and validity issues have led to calls from professional educational organizations for protection against high-stakes decisions based on results from single tests or assessments (American Educational Research Association, 2000). The *Standards for Educational and Psychological Testing* (American Educational Research Association, American Psychological Association, & National Council on Measurement in Education, 1999) specifically state, "In educational settings, a decision or characterization that will have major impact on a student should not be made on the basis of a single test score. Other relevant information should be taken into account if it will enhance the overall validity of the decision" (pp. 147–148). Similarly, the *Standards for Professional Learning* (Learning Forward, 2011) emphasize, "Data from multiple sources enrich decisions about professional learning that leads to increased results for every student. . . . The use of multiple sources of data offers a balanced and more comprehensive analysis of student, educator, and system performance than any single type or source of data can" (pp. 4–5).

Yet despite these appeals, the exclusive use of large-scale assessment results for making decisions about schools, students, and even professional learning remains widespread (Barton, 2002; Hess, 2005; Kifer, 2001). In some contexts, however, the use of multiple measures appears to be gaining ground. Title I of the Elementary and Secondary Education Act (ESEA), for example, stipulates that multiple measures should be used to evaluate schools with respect to their academic standards. The rationales for using multiple measures include providing a fuller representation of student and teacher performance; providing a more adequate, and thus more equitable, representation of the many ways teachers interpret content; and providing individual students with more, and thus fairer, opportunities to demonstrate competence (Baker, 2003). From a technical perspective, the use of multiple measures also serves to reduce measurement error and thus improve the quality and validity of the decisions made (Henderson-Montero, Julian, & Yen, 2003).

A number of formats for using multiple measures have been proposed in recent years (see Chester, 2003), the most common being the provision of multiple opportunities for students to take assessments or for teachers to demonstrate skills, especially when results are used as a basis for making high-stakes decisions. Other formats include the use of more than one assessment measure within the same or different content areas (e.g., language arts, mathematics, and science), the use of different types of assessment information (e.g., norm referenced, criterion referenced, performance assessments, teacher-developed assessments, and portfolio assessments), and the use of assessments with different item types (selected response, constructed response, and performance events). Multiple measures also can include non-cognitive indices such as attendance, class participation, and dropout or persistence rates (Henderson-Montero et al., 2003).

Using multiple measures to judge the quality of educators' professional learning can be a highly complex process, however. Difficult decisions must be made about the number and types of measures to include and the methods that will be used to combine that information (Koretz, 2003; Schafer, 2003). Nevertheless, growing evidence demonstrates that thoughtful decisions regarding these procedures can lead to more reliable and more defensible judgments (see Henderson-Montero et al., 2003; National Research Council, 1999).

Concerns about the fairness and defensibility of making decisions about the quality of professional learning undoubtedly will lead to increased calls for the use of multiple sources of data and to the development of better models for combining different sources of data. Information on the psychometric properties of the various measures considered will be vital in these efforts. So too will be information about how various stakeholders regard the different measures of success. In other words, in choosing what measures to include, policy makers may want to consider what sources of evidence educators believe provide the most valid depiction of professional learning quality (see Guskey, 2012).

Despite widespread agreement about the need to use multiple measures for making decisions about schools, students, and professional learning, no clear consensus exists about what specific measures should be used, the most appropriate methods for synthesizing that evidence, or the most effective procedures for communicating that information to the public (Henderson-Montero et al., 2003). The psychometric quality of various measures, particularly the reliability and validity of inferences made, should be a major factor in selecting specific indicators for use in making these high-stakes decisions (see Popham, 2006). But various stakeholders' perceptions of the validity of different measures may be an important consideration as well.

Other research has shown, for example, that individuals' perceptions of the meaningfulness and relevance of assessment results affect the motivation and effort they put forth to improve instruction and student learning outcomes (Lane, Parke, & Stone, 1998). If school administrators and teachers differ in their perceptions of the meaningfulness, validity, and relevancy of these different sources of evidence on student learning, for example, then it seems imperative those sources of evidence be expanded. Minimally they should include indicators of student learning that are trusted and believed by individuals who are key stakeholders in the improvement process and for whom the consequences of accountability are most significant (Guskey, 2007b). Specifically, they should include sources of evidence directly relevant to teachers and to their classroom activities.

BEGIN WITH THE GOALS

The goals of professional learning describe what we hope to accomplish and set forth the criteria by which success will be judged. As we stated at the beginning, the goal of professional learning is to increase "educator effectiveness and results for all students" (Learning Forward, 2011). In this sense, goals are not something to consider only at the end when activities are completed. Instead, they must be where we begin planning all professional learning endeavors (Guskey, 2001a, 2001b, 2002a, 2005b, 2007a).

As Covey (2004) reminded us, we must always "begin with the end in mind." Before thinking about the content or format of any professional learning, planners must first consider the goals they hope to accomplish. This requires addressing two essential questions: What goals do we want to achieve, especially with regard to student learning, and what data best reflect the achievement of those goals? These two questions should mark the starting point in all planning discussions.

Deciding what goals we want to achieve typically involves careful analysis of current data on student learning and the teaching and learning context. Results from large-scale state assessments and nationally normed standardized exams may be important for accountability purposes and need to be included (Brennan, Kim, Wenz-Gross, & Siperstein, 2001). School administrators generally consider these to be valid indicators of success. Teachers, however, see limitations in large-scale assessment data. These assessments are generally administered only once a year, and results may not be available until several months later. By that time, the school year may have ended and students promoted to another teacher's class. So, while these assessments are important, many teachers do not find such data particularly useful (Guskey, 2007b).

Teachers put more trust in results from their own assessments of student learning: classroom assessments, common formative assessments (Ainsworth & Viegut, 2006), and portfolios of student work. They turn to these sources of data for feedback to determine if the new strategies or practices they are implementing really make a difference. Classroom assessments provide timely, targeted, and instructionally relevant data that also can be used to plan revisions when needed. Classroom observations and discussions with students often help pinpoint areas of concern. Interviews with teachers, focus groups, or discussions in professional learning communities (DuFour, 2004) are especially valuable when trying to identify persistent trouble spots in efforts to help all students succeed in mastering complex concepts and skills. Since teachers comprise a major stakeholder group in any professional learning endeavor, sources of data that they trust and believe will be particularly important to include (Guskey, 2012).

Furthermore, while data on student academic achievement will always be essential, affective and behavioral indicators of student performance can be relevant as well. These include student surveys designed to measure how much students like school; their perceptions of teachers, fellow students, and themselves; their sense of self-efficacy; and their confidence in new learning situations. Data from school records on attendance, enrollment patterns, dropout rates, class disruptions, and disciplinary actions are also important. In some areas, parents' or families' perceptions may be a vital consideration. This is especially true in initiatives that involve changes in grading practices, report cards, or other aspects of school-to-home and home-to-school communication (Epstein & Associates, 2009; Guskey, 2002c; Guskey & Bailey, 2001, 2010).

Analyzing the performance of subgroups of students can bring additional insights to these discussions. Considering the learning progress of students of different backgrounds and ability levels, language experiences, ethnicity, race, and gender can be particularly informative. Looking at differences between classrooms and between schools often yields new understandings of problem areas as well.

The key point in these discussions is to ensure that the focus remains on "educator effectiveness and results for all students" (Learning Forward, 2011). Because of concerns about professional learning processes, conversations often skip to the content and activities in which participating educators will be involved. We begin debating new ideas, strategies, innovations, programs, and instructional technologies. While these are important issues, we must remember that they are means to an important end that must be determined first. After deciding the specific desired goals with regard to student learning, decisions about the most appropriate means will be much easier to make.

THE IMPORTANCE OF TRANSPARENCY IN GATHERING DATA

The procedures used to gather data always must be explicit and transparent. Just as students should never be surprised by the evidence used to evaluate their performance, educators should not be surprised by the data selected to measure the outcomes of their professional learning. Not only should they know what those sources of data will be, but they should have a voice in choosing them.

The best way to ensure transparency is to define the goals and address questions about what data best reflect those goals during the initial planning process. Deciding at the start what data best show achievement of a particular goal brings purpose and direction to professional learning. Involving different stakeholders in deciding what data to use and in gathering that evidence further guarantees results will be seen as credible and trustworthy. It also reinforces the idea that improvement is an ongoing process that requires input and collaboration among all stakeholders.

TYPES OF DATA

As is evident in our discussion thus far, there are many different types of data. We typically distinguish these various types of data by their *form* and by their *function* or *purpose*. In other words, we classify data first according to its structure and second based on how it is used. Although these classifications are never exact, and overlap among categories frequently occurs, they are helpful in clarifying specific characteristics of the data and explaining its meaning in specific contexts.

Data Forms

In essence, data come in two basic forms: quantitative and qualitative. These forms differ in their structure, the way they are recorded, and the methods used in their analysis.

Quantitative data are typically derived from measures of traits or characteristics that are recorded as numeric values. Some quantitative data serve simply to label different categories. These are referred to as "nominal" data in which numbers are used only to distinguish one category from another. We might, for example, label female teachers as "1" and male teachers as "2." Or we might use numbers to distinguish students of different background characteristics, race, or ethnicity.

Other quantitative data represent counts that can have only whole number values and are referred to as "discrete" data. Examples include the number of days a student is absent from school, the number of children enrolled in a school, and the number of years of teaching experience a teacher has.

Still other quantitative data result from measuring traits directly with some type of measurement tool specifically designed for that purpose. Because these measures can take on any range of values they are referred to as "continuous" data. We might, for example, measure students' weight using a scale or their height using a tape measure. We also could measure the time teachers spend in collaborative planning or the amount of money a school spends on a particular professional learning activity.

Much of the quantitative data we use in education, however, come from indirect measures. We cannot, for example, directly measure traits such as students' achievement in mathematics or teachers' skill in implementing a particular instructional technique. So instead, we create a series of questions that require students to show their achievement or tasks that require teachers to demonstrate their skill. We then assign a numerical value or "score" to how well students answer the questions or teachers perform the tasks.

Quantitative data typically are analyzed through statistical procedures and summarized using statistics like averages (central tendency), measures of variation (spread), and correlations (association). The accuracy of quantitative data depends on the precision of the measuring device. Some traits or characteristics can be measured accurately, such as demographics, financial resources, attendance, disciplinary actions, graduation rates, and participation in school-sponsored extracurricular programs. Measures of other traits or characteristics, however, especially those measured indirectly, are subject to greater measurement error and must be interpreted more cautiously. Examples would include measures of students' attitudes, dispositions, and achievement, or teachers' beliefs, perceptions, and performance.

Qualitative data represent information that is not numerical in form. These data may be gathered from observations, reflections, interviews, self-reports, open-ended questionnaires, or surveys. Qualitative data are typically descriptive in nature and, as such, are harder to analyze. They are used most often in studies or evaluations at an individual person or institution (i.e., school or district) level. Many case studies yield qualitative data where the focus is on providing rich and in-depth information about a particular context rather than on findings that might be generalized to other contexts.

Analyzing qualitative data can be difficult because it requires accurate, detailed descriptions of both participants and their responses. This usually involves sorting responses to open-ended questions and interviews into broad themes, labeling those themes, and then interpreting the meaning for that particular context. Quotations from personal reflections or interviews might be used to illustrate points made in the analysis. Expert knowledge of an area is often necessary in interpreting qualitative data, and great care must be taken in the analysis so as not to bias the results.

Many reports and investigations yield both quantitative and qualitative data, sometimes generated from the same instrument or measurement tool. Questionnaires and surveys, for example, produce numerical data from summaries of responses (e.g., "yes" and "no" answers or rating scale responses). But the same questionnaire or survey might ask participants to explain their responses, offer examples, or tell why they responded in a particular way, yielding qualitative data.

What is important to recognize is that the appropriateness of any set of data rests not in its form but in its pertinence to the specific question or questions it is used to answer. As we stressed earlier, specific, essential questions always must come first. These questions guide selection of the most meaningful form of data needed to answer those questions. To say that one wants to gather either quantitative or qualitative data, without having articulated the questions to be addressed, is both foolish and unthinking.

Data Purposes

Another way in which we distinguish data is by its *function* or *purpose;* that is, by how it is used. Because the appropriate use of data comes from the essential questions being addressed, those questions again become central to the discussion of function or purpose.

Most data serve one of two purposes: formative or summative. It frequently occurs, however, that the same data can serve either or both of these purposes. For this reason, the essential questions addressed become a more important factor in determining the data's purpose than the nature of the data itself.

Formative data basically describe and inform. They may depict context, conditions, participants, actions, or interactions. Formative data may be historical, descriptive of current status, or predictive of future trends. They may be quantitative or qualitative. They can be used to diagnose problems or to identify strengths.

Essentially, formative data describe what is going on and, in some cases, offer explanations as to why. Examples include information about teachers' engagement in professional learning; the content and format of those activities; students' perceptions, achievement, behavior, and discipline; participation in extracurricular programs; and post-graduation education. Such information can be useful in understanding students' backgrounds and learning needs, particularly if they are analyzed in relation to specific student characteristics.

Summative data are used to make judgments and evaluations. They provide information about what was accomplished, what the consequences were (positive and negative), what the final results were (intended and unintended), and, in some cases, whether the benefits justify the costs (P. Phillips, 2002).

The primary purpose of summative data is to provide pertinent information to guide decisions about a policy, program, or activity's overall merit or worth. It is information decision makers can use to make crucial decisions about all aspects of professional learning. Should a particular activity be continued as is? Continued with modifications? Expanded? Discontinued? Ultimately, the focus of summative data is the policy, program, or activity's overall value and impact; that is, "the bottom line."

Perhaps the best description of the distinction between formative and summative data is one offered by Robert Stake: "When the cook tastes the soup, that's formative; when the guests taste the soup, that's summative" (quoted in Scriven, 1991, p. 169).

TYPES OF STUDENT LEARNING GOALS AND DATA

Because the *Standards for Professional Learning* focus on improving "results for all students" (Learning Forward, 2011), student learning goals and data are a vital consideration in all professional learning endeavors. Data related to student learning in education have long been classified in three broad domains: *cognitive, affective,* and *psychomotor.*

Cognitive Data

Cognitive goals (Bloom, Englehart, Furst, Hill, & Krathwohl, 1956) provide the basis of most forms of academic achievement and come first to mind when we think about the purposes of formal education. Data related to cognitive goals describe the concepts and skills students have gained as a result of planned instructional activities. Cognitive goals also provide the foundation of every school's academic curriculum. Although some cognitive goals apply across multiple content areas (e.g., problem solving and critical thinking), most data on cognitive goals are subject area specific. Hence, "student learning in language arts" may be distinct from "student learning in mathematics" or "student learning in science."

The curriculums of most countries throughout the world consider a broad range of cognitive goals in different content areas.

Evidence showing achievement of those goals thus requires a variety of sources of cognitive data. Australia's national curriculum, for example, focuses on reading, spelling, writing and numeracy skills, as well as science literacy, civics and citizenship, and information and communication technology (Ministerial Council on Education, Employment, Training and Youth Affairs, 2006). In Japan the Education Ministry highlights creating well-rounded students in the national curriculum by emphasizing subjects such as music, arts and handicrafts, and homemaking, physical education, and moral education, as well as math and science. Their curriculum also devotes a large amount of time to Japanese language and life activities that give younger students personal life experiences in preparation for classroom-oriented science. In life activities class, students participate in activities such as picking flowers, raising rabbits, catching frogs and insects, and watching falling stars (Wu, 1999).

Furthermore, because cognitive goals span a broad range of subdomains and topics in each subject area, student learning data within a subject area can vary in its breadth. The *Common Core State Standards Initiative* (CCSSO, 2010) in the United States, for example, divides student learning goals (standards) in language arts into the subdomains of Reading, Writing, Speaking/Listening, and Language. Mathematics subdomains consist of Operations and Algebraic Thinking, Number and Operations—Base Ten, Number and Operations—Fractions, Measurement and Data, Geometry, and Mathematical Practices. Researchers concerned with the content validity of measures of student learning data in a subject area must ensure adequate sampling of concepts and skills across these subdomains (Sireci, 1998).

Within each subdomain, cognitive goals also can vary in intellectual complexity or depth. They can range from simple goals that require only recall of factual information, to more complex goals that call for sophisticated reasoning and higher mental processes, such as the ability to make applications, analyze relationships, or draw inferences. Recent criticism of mathematics instruction in the United States, for example, focused on these issues of depth. Noting that U.S. teachers tend to cover a wider range of topics than do teachers in other developed countries, but explore few topics in great depth, researchers described the U.S. mathematics curriculum as "a mile wide and an inch deep" (Duffrin, 1998). The current emphasis on *21st Century Skills* (Larson & Miller, 2011) comes largely from concerns about the lack of depth in many established curriculums.

Affective Data

Affective goals (Krathwohl, Bloom, & Masia, 1964) refer to students' attitudes, interests, feelings, beliefs, and dispositions. They relate to how students feel and what they believe about the subjects they are studying, their teachers, school, learning, and themselves as learners. Affective goals also relate to the development of responsibility, consideration, empathy, respect for others, self-confidence, motivation, and self-regulation. Data related to affective learning goals typically come from teacher observations or from surveys or questionnaires administered to students.

Some researchers, teachers, and parents believe that affective learning goals are just as important as cognitive goals, although they seldom hold the same prominence in school curriculums (Guskey & Anderman, 2008). Affective goals tend to be emphasized more in elementary grades than in secondary grades, and student report cards at the elementary level often include teachers' evaluations of students' achievement of specific affective goals (Guskey & Bailey, 2010).

Psychomotor Data

Psychomotor goals (Simpson, 1966), often referred to as "behavioral" goals, typically require student performances or demonstrations of specific skills or behaviors. In certain fields, like the performing arts and physical education, these skills and behaviors are the focus of instruction and a vital aspect of student achievement. In other instances psychomotor goals involve student learning behaviors such as participation or engagement, attendance, persistence, punctuality, cooperation, work habits, and effort. The life activities in the Japanese curriculum described earlier reflect largely psychomotor goals. Data on psychomotor goals most often come from teacher observations and evaluations of students' performance using carefully articulated rubrics. In some cases, however, such data can come from observations made by classmates or students' self-evaluations.

RELATIONSHIPS AMONG TYPES OF GOALS AND DATA

Over the years researchers have debated the relations among the cognitive, affective, and psychomotor goals and the data that represent their achievement. Studies consistently yield positive but moderate correlations among measures of student learning in each domain (e.g., Knuver & Brandsma, 1993), but cause-and-effect relations have been difficult to confirm. Some researchers consider affective and psychomotor goals to be "enabling" traits or behaviors that facilitate student achievement of cognitive outcomes (McMillan, 2001). Students with interest in the content, confidence in their ability to learn, and who actively engage in instructional activities, for example, tend to perform well on associated cognitive tasks. Other researchers contend, however, that cognitive results prompt affective and psychomotor responses. Students who succeed on cognitive tasks tend to like the content, experience increased confidence, and are more likely to engage in subsequent, related learning experiences (Creemers & Kyriakides, 2010). Significant differences among students in these relations are also known to exist. The best that can be said, therefore, is that measures of student learning in these three domains and the data that result from those measures tend to be moderately related, and those relations appear to be reciprocal.

LEVELS OF DATA

Educators collect and analyze data at a variety of levels. The type and form of data gathered at each level can be the same or may be different, depending on the goals and the questions being addressed. What remains crucial is that the goals and related questions always come first. As we have emphasized throughout, data become meaningful and valuable *only* when processed for the purpose of answering specific questions.

Classroom Data

Since our primary goal in professional learning is to improve results for all students, the most important level of data to consider is that closest to students: the classroom level. And among the various sources of data available at the classroom level, undoubtedly the most important is the information teachers gather from classroom assessments.

"Assessment" is one of those common terms in education that everyone uses but few people define in exactly the same way. Some educators argue that "assessment" is simply the more modern word for "testing." Others contend that it implies something much more.

In the context of education, assessment is a *process* for gathering and interpreting information for use in making decisions about students, instruction, curriculums, programs, and educational policies (see American Federation of Teachers, National Council on Measurement in Education, & National Education Association, 1990).

From this definition, we can see that assessment in education refers to more than simply administering, scoring, and grading tests. It includes the broad range of strategies and techniques that educators use to understand students better and to monitor the effects of instructional programs and policies. As such, assessment can certainly involve quizzes and larger examinations composed of multiple-choice and constructed-response items that are administered in pencil-and-paper form or online. But it also includes classroom observations, interviews, compositions, oral presentations, skill demonstrations, projects, reports, experiments, notebooks, journals, exhibits of students' work, and paper or digital portfolios (Russell & Airasian, 2011).

Teachers make a wide variety of decisions on the basis of classroom assessment data. Perhaps most important is the use of assessment results to determine the effectiveness of different teaching strategies, classroom activities, and instructional materials. With these data teachers can make better decisions about what to maintain and what needs to be changed or improved. Data gathered from classroom assessments also helps teachers determine who is learning well, who is struggling, and what specific difficulties struggling students are experiencing. It gives teachers direction in developing instructional alternatives for those students who are having problems and for planning extension or enrichment activities for students who have learned well. Moreover, it allows teachers to make better decisions when planning next steps in instruction for individual students and for the entire class.

Teachers also consider classroom assessment data when placing students into various educational programs, assigning appropriate grades, counseling students, selecting them for educational interventions or opportunities, and credentialing or certifying students' competence. Data from assessments inform decisions about the effectiveness of different curriculums and how to improve them. In addition, assessment data provide the basis for making decisions about educational policies at the classroom, school, district, state, and national levels (Nitko & Brookhart, 2010). In essence, classroom assessment data provide vital information about all aspects of student learning; that is, what students know, are able to do, and believe at a particular point in time.

School Data

Moving from the classroom level to the school level of data takes a step away from direct contact and involvement with students. But many important questions regarding professional learning are school based. School leaders might consider data about school resources such as financial support, available technology, personnel assignments, and time allocations. School staffs might look at participation in school activities, levels of engagement, types of communication, collaborative planning, and parent involvement. In addition, school policies related to scheduling, attendance, discipline, and grading and reporting can have a powerful influence on students and teachers alike.

When it comes to analyzing data from assessments of student learning at the school level, the most important and most helpful information for guiding improvement comes not from statistics like averages or overall scores. It also does not come from comparisons of a school's results with averages from the state, province, or nation. Rather, it comes from exploring and analyzing variation in students' responses to individual items or subsections of items on the assessment. Consider the following example from Guskey and Jung (2013) based on the analysis of data gathered by the teachers in one school from the administration of a common formative assessment.

Increasing numbers of educators today are discovering the advantages of "common" formative assessments. These assessments can vary widely in their form and structure, as can any type of assessment. What makes them different is that they are collaboratively developed, scored, and analyzed by teams of teachers rather than by an individual teacher (Ainsworth & Viegut, 2006). These teacher teams usually have similar grade-level assignments or teach in the same academic department in a school.

To develop common formative assessments, teacher teams first examine the standards or learning goals for each instructional unit and then collaboratively develop assessments that they believe will capture how well students have mastered those standards or goals. Some teams work directly from curriculum frameworks, guides, or maps, while others use "Tables of Specification" (Guskey, 2005a). Team members administer these collaboratively developed formative assessments in their individual classes at about the same time. They then get together to analyze the results and plan corrective activities when needed.

For many teams, the first step in their analysis is to construct a table like the one illustrated in Figure 1.1. This table shows a tally of how many students in each teacher's class answered each item incorrectly or failed to meet a particular performance criterion. These simple tallies reveal several important findings. Specifically,

A. All students answered items 4 and 8 correctly. Generally this is a wonderful result indicating that the standards to which these items or prompts relate were taught so well by all three teachers that all students were able to demonstrate their mastery. It also may be, however, that these items or prompts were structured in way that revealed the correct response or made the correct answer obvious. If inspection confirms that this is true, then the teachers will need to revise these items or prompts on the assessment.

B. Most students in all three teachers' classes did well on items 1, 2, 5, 6, 10, and 11. This shows that the instructional practices the teachers used in teaching these particular standards worked well for nearly all students and should be continued. Only a few students in each teacher's class will need to revisit these standards and continue to work on mastery.

C. Although many students in Jen's class struggled with item 3, most students in Michael's and Chris's classes answered this item correctly. In this case, Michael and Chris might offer Jen advice on how she could revise her instructional strategies for this particular standard or goal.

D. For item 7, most of Jen's students did very well but the majority of students in Michael's and Chris's classes had difficulty. Jen can share how she approached this topic or standard and the strategies she used to engage her students. This could help Michael and Chris develop more effective strategies for teaching this particular standard. Similarly for item 12, Michael's approach appears to have led to greater success than that of Jen or Chris.

Figure 1.1   Analysis of Items Answered Incorrectly by Students on a Common Formative Assessment

Formative Assessment 3			
Item	Jen	Michael	Chris
1							
2								
3	### ### ###								
4			
5										
6									
7				### ###					### ### ###	
8			
9	### ### ###		### ###					
10										
11							
12	###						### ###
13	### ### ###	|||| ### ### ||	### ### |||
14					###		###
15	###			###	###	

Source: Guskey & Jung, 2013. Copyright © 2013 Corwin. Used with permission.

E. Items 13, 14, and 15 address standards that continue to be problems for students in all three teachers classes, especially the standard associated with item 13. When this occurs and if the items are found to be appropriate, teachers need to seek solutions outside of their individual experiences and expertise. They might consult an instructional coach, critical friend/coach, district coordinator, teachers in other schools, or other subject area experts. They might explore research evidence on effective instructional practices related to these particular standards or goals. They might consider alternative instructional approaches or activities presented in other materials, teaching guides, or online sources. Because these problems are shared by all three teachers, it's clear they will need to turn to resources other than each other to find effective solutions.

The purpose of this kind of data analysis is to help all of the teachers involved to improve the quality of their instruction so that all of their students learn well. Of course, teachers need to have the necessary time and resources to conduct these kinds of analyses and to develop instructional alternatives. This means that school leaders need to find creative ways to adjust daily teaching schedules so that teachers can meet to do this important work.

With appropriate guidance, the collaborative preparation of common formative assessments assists teachers in developing better assessment tools. But the most vital aspect of this process is the analysis of results and how teachers use the results to revise their instructional strategies and techniques. Working with colleagues in a supportive environment for the collective benefit of all, teachers can be valuable resources to one another in their improvement efforts. Together they can develop better formative assessments that provide students with higher-quality feedback on their learning. Such collaboration also helps teachers create and implement more varied and more effective instructional alternatives so that more students learn well.

It is precisely this form of data analysis, looking for variation in students' responses among classrooms, that can provide the basis for making specific, targeted improvements that help improve learning for all students.

District or Jurisdiction Data

Data summarized at the district or jurisdiction level take us another step away from direct contact and involvement with students. Yet because many school policies are established at the district or jurisdiction level, data gathered at this level can be particularly useful.

Like school-level data, the most meaningful analysis of the district or jurisdiction data comes from the exploration of variation, particularly among schools. Are all schools comparably successful in some areas? If so, such evidence offers support for the effectiveness of professional learning endeavors in these areas. Are there other areas where all schools appear to be struggling? If that is the case, then it appears efforts to date have not worked well and need to be revised or abandoned completely for other strategies.

It also may be discovered in comparing data from schools within the district or jurisdiction that school results vary; that is, some schools are doing quite well in particular areas while others are showing little progress. Such results should lead to important conversations as to possible reasons behind such variation.

It may be that the schools vary in context and those contextual differences influence results. Perhaps the schools serve different student populations in communities with different demographic characteristics, and those characteristics have some influence on results. Policies or strategies that work well in one context often work less well in other contexts. It also may be that differences in school leadership, faculty experience, or school structure account for the difference.

If some schools have found ways to be successful, however, it may be that the processes and procedures they used to gain that success can be shared with schools that are struggling. In other words, models of excellence may exist that are close by. Developing structured professional learning opportunities that allow these successful processes and procedures to be shared in a nonthreatening, collaborative environment could prove exceptionally powerful.

State, Provincial, or National Data

Analysis of data at the state, provincial, or national level is useful primarily for addressing large-scale policy questions. Again, inspection of the variation that exists among states, provinces, or nations can be helpful in answering questions about policy at this level. But context differences that might exert strong influence on results also must be kept in mind.

ATTAINMENT VERSUS IMPROVEMENT STUDENT DATA

Another important distinction in gathering and analyzing data on student learning is between "attainment" and "improvement" data. "Attainment" data describe students' level of achievement at a particular point in time. It provides a time-specific snapshot of what students have accomplished. Individual measures of attainment may be interpreted in comparison to the performance on the same items or tasks of a large, normative group of students who are similar in age or at the same grade level. When we say that a student is "on grade level" or "scored at the 60th percentile," we are making these kinds of "norm-referenced" comparisons.

Attainment measures also may be described in terms of the particular learning criteria that students have met at a grade level or in a specific course of study. Such "criterion-referenced" comparisons are used when we say that a student has "reached proficiency" or has "met grade-level expectations." Attainment data provided the basis for accountability in the American No Child Left Behind Act, which required schools to record the percentage of students in various subgroups at each grade level that reached a predetermined level of proficiency on state assessments.

"Improvement" data describe what a student or group of students gain as a result of their learning experiences in school. Because it is based on documented change in performance, improvement requires two, parallel or "linked" measures of student learning: one administered at the beginning of an instructional sequence and another at the end. Measures of improvement provide the basis for "growth trajectories" in education and "value-added" models of accountability (Martineau, 2010).

Most educators assume that attainment and improvement measures of student achievement would be comparable because both are based on the similar assessment results. But the relation between measures of attainment and improvement tends to be quite modest (Weiss 2008). Certain students might make significant learning progress and improve greatly on measures of their achievement during an academic term, but still not reach the predetermined level of proficiency expected for their grade level or course. Students with learning disabilities and those from disadvantaged backgrounds frequently fall into this category (see Jung & Guskey, 2012). Other students, especially those with exceptional ability, may attain the same high level of performance on initial and final measures of their achievement but demonstrate little or no improvement. Thus examining attainment and improvement data might yield very different conclusions about what students have achieved.

EVALUATING PROFESSIONAL LEARNING

Finally, data play a major role in evaluating professional learning endeavors. Well-designed evaluations provide the information needed to increase professional learning quality and effectiveness. They also provide useful evidence for those who advocate for professional learning; those responsible for engaging in, planning, facilitating, or supporting professional learning; and those who want to know about the contribution of professional learning to student achievement.

As we noted earlier, educators' professional learning experiences cover a broad range of activities. Many of those experiences involve informal, personal reflections on the everyday interactions between teachers and students. Teachers regularly try new approaches to instruction, gather information to learn how well those approaches work for their students, and then decide what changes need to be made or what instructional alternatives might be considered to improve students' learning success. Thoughtful deliberations on these ongoing classroom interactions are a vital part of every teacher's professional learning.

In addition to these informal reflections, school leaders and teachers also take part in a variety of more structured professional learning experiences specifically designed to enhance their knowledge and improve their professional skills. These experiences include not only the broad spectrum of seminars and workshops in which educators engage, but also online programs, peer observations, professional learning communities, coaching or mentoring, university courses, conferences, and the like. Our focus here is on evaluating the effects of these more structured and formalized professional learning endeavors.

The Need for Sound Evaluations

Many educators see evaluating professional learning as a costly, time-consuming process that diverts attention from important planning, implementation, and follow-up activities. Others believe that they simply lack the skill and expertise needed to become involved in rigorous evaluations. As a result they either ignore evaluation issues completely, or leave them to "evaluation experts" who are called in at the end and asked to determine if what was done made any difference. Sadly, these last-minute, post hoc evaluation efforts are seldom adequate in determining any experience or activity's true effects.

Good evaluations of professional learning, however, do not have to be costly or complicated. What they require is thoughtful planning, the ability to ask good questions, and a basic understanding of how to collect appropriate data in order to find valid answers. In many ways, good evaluations are merely the refinement of everyday thinking. They provide sound, meaningful, and sufficiently reliable information that allows thoughtful and responsible decisions to be made about professional learning processes and effects.

The Meaning of "Evaluation"

Just as there are many forms of professional learning, there are also many forms of evaluation. While experts may disagree on the best definition of evaluation, a useful operational definition for most purposes is this: *Evaluation is the systematic investigation of merit or worth* (adapted from the Joint Committee on Standards for Educational Evaluation, 1994).

Each part of this definition holds special significance. The word "systematic" distinguishes this process from the multitude of informal evaluation acts in which people consciously engage. Systematic implies that evaluation in this context is thoughtful, intentional, and purposeful. It is done for clear reasons and with explicit intent. Although its specific purpose may vary from one setting to another, all good evaluations are organized and deliberate.

Because it is systematic, some educators mistakenly believe that professional learning evaluation is appropriate only for planned seminars and workshops, but not for the wide range of other less structured, ongoing, job-embedded professional learning activities. Regardless of the form it takes, however, professional learning is not a haphazard process. It is, or should be, purposeful and results- or goal-driven (Schmoker, 2004, 2006). Its objectives remain clear: to make a positive difference in teaching, to help educators reach high standards, and ultimately, to have a positive impact on students. This is true of seminars and workshops, as well as study groups, professional learning communities, action research, collaborative planning, curriculum development, structured observations, peer coaching and mentoring, and individually guided professional learning activities. To determine if the goals of these activities are met, or if progress is being made, requires systematic evaluation.

"Investigation" refers to collecting and analyzing appropriate and pertinent information. While no evaluation can be completely objective, the process is not founded on opinion or conjecture. Rather, it is based on acquiring specific, relevant, and valid evidence examined through appropriate methods and techniques.

Using "merit or worth" in the definition implies appraisal and judgment. Evaluations are designed to determine something's value. They help answer questions such as these:

- Is this experience or activity leading to the intended results?
- Is it better than what was done in the past?
- Is it better than another, competing activity?
- Is it worth the costs?

Answers to these questions require more than a statement of findings. They demand an appraisal of quality and judgments of value, based on the best data available.

The Critical Levels of Professional Learning Evaluation

Effective professional learning evaluation requires consideration of the five critical stages or levels of information shown in Figure 1.2 (Guskey, 2000a, 2002a, 2005b). These five levels represent an adaptation of an evaluation model developed by Kirkpatrick (1959, 1998) for judging the value of supervisory training programs in business and industry. Kirkpatrick's model, although widely applied, has seen limited use in education because of inadequate explanatory power. While helpful in addressing a broad range of "what" questions, many find it lacking when it comes to explaining "why" (Alliger & Janak, 1989; Holton, 1996).

The five levels in this model are hierarchically arranged, from simple to more complex. With each succeeding level, the process of gathering evaluation data requires more time and resources. And because each level builds on those that come before, success at one level is usually necessary for success at higher levels.

Level 1: Participants' Reactions. The first level of evaluation looks at participants' reactions to the professional learning experience. This is the most common form of professional learning evaluation and the easiest type of data to gather and analyze.

Figure 1.2 Five Levels of Professional Learning Evaluation

Evaluation Level	What Questions Are Addressed?	How Will Data Be Gathered?	What Is Measured or Assessed?	How Will Data Be Used?
1. Participants' Reactions	• Did they like it? • Was their time well spent? • Did the material make sense? • Will it be useful? • Was the leader knowledgeable and helpful? • Were the refreshments fresh and tasty? • Was the room the right temperature? • Were the chairs comfortable?	• Questionnaires or surveys administered at the end of the session	• Initial satisfaction with the experience	• To improve program design and delivery
2. Participants' Learning	• Did participants acquire the intended knowledge and skills?	• Paper-and-pencil instruments • Simulations • Demonstrations • Participant reflections (oral and/or written) • Participant portfolios	• New knowledge and skills of participants	• To improve program content, format, and organization
3. Organizational Support & Change	• Were sufficient resources made available? • Were problems addressed quickly and efficiently? • Was implementation advocated, facilitated, and supported? • Were successes recognized and shared?	• Minutes from follow-up meetings • Questionnaires • Structured interviews with participants and district or school administrators • District and school records • Participant portfolios	• The organization's advocacy, support, accommodation, facilitation, and recognition	• To document and improve organizational support • To inform future change efforts

Evaluation Level	What Questions Are Addressed?	How Will Data Be Gathered?	What Is Measured or Assessed?	How Will Data Be Used?
	• Was the support public and overt? • What was the impact on the organization? • Did it affect organizational climate and procedures?			
4. Participants' Use of New Knowledge and Skills	• Did participants effectively apply the new knowledge and skills?	• Questionnaires • Structured interviews with participants and their supervisors • Participant reflections (oral and/or written) • Participant portfolios • Direct observations • Video or audio recordings	• Degree and quality of implementation	• To document and improve the implementation of program content

5. Student Learning Outcomes	• What was the impact on students?
	 • Did it affect student performance or achievement?
	 • Did it influence students' physical or emotional well-being?
	 • Are students more confident as learners?
	 • Is student attendance improving?
	 • Are dropouts decreasing?
		• Student records
		 • School records
		 • Questionnaires
		 • Structured interviews with students, parents, teachers, and/or administrators
		 • Participant portfolios
			• Student learning outcomes:
			   ○ Cognitive (performance & achievement)
			   ○ Affective (attitudes & dispositions)
			   ○ Psychomotor (skills & behaviors)
				• To focus and improve all aspects of program design, implementation, and follow-up
				 • To demonstrate the overall impact of professional development

Source: Guskey, 2000a. Copyright © 2000 Thomas R. Guskey. Used with permission.

At Level 1 the questions addressed focus on whether or not participants liked the experience. Did they feel their time was well spent? Did the content and material make sense to them? Were the activities well planned and meaningful? Was the leader knowledgeable, credible, and helpful? Did they find the information useful?

Also important for some professional learning experiences are questions related to the context: Was the room the right temperature? Were the chairs comfortable? Were the refreshments fresh and tasty? To some, questions such as these may seem silly and inconsequential. But experienced professional development leaders know the importance of attending to these basic human needs.

Data on participants' reactions are usually gathered through questionnaires handed out at the end of a program or activity, or by online surveys distributed later through e-mail. These questionnaires and surveys typically include a combination of rating-scale items and open-ended response questions that allow participants to provide more personalized comments. Because of the general nature of this information, many organizations use the same questionnaire or survey for all of their professional learning activities, regardless of the format.

Some educators refer to these measures of participants' reactions as "happiness quotients," insisting that they reveal only the entertainment value of an experience or activity, not its quality or worth. But measuring participants' initial satisfaction provides data that can help improve the design and delivery of professional learning programs or activities in valid ways. In addition, positive reactions from participants are usually a necessary prerequisite to higher-level evaluation results.

Level 2: Participants' Learning. In addition to liking their professional learning experiences, participants ought to learn something from them. Level 2 focuses on measuring the new knowledge, skills, and perhaps attitudes or dispositions that participants gain (Guskey, 2002b). Depending on the goals of the professional learning program or activity, this can involve anything from a pencil-and-paper assessment (Can participants describe the critical attributes of effective questioning techniques and give examples of how these might be applied in common classroom situations?) to a simulation or full-scale skill demonstration (Presented with a variety of classroom conflicts, can participants diagnose each situation, and then prescribe and carry out a fair and workable solution?). Oral or written personal reflections or examinations of the portfolios participants assemble also can be used to document their learning.

Although Level 2 evaluation data often can be gathered at the completion of a professional learning program or activity, it usually requires more than a standardized form. And because measures must show attainment of specific learning goals, indicators of successful learning need to be outlined *before* activities begin.

Careful evaluators also consider possible "unintended" learning outcomes, both positive and negative. Professional learning activities that engage teachers and school leaders in collaboration, for example, can additionally foster a positive sense of community and shared purpose among participants (Supovitz, 2002). But in some instances, individuals collaborate to block change or inhibit advancement (Corcoran, Fuhrman, & Belcher, 2001; Little, 1990). Investigations further show that collaborative efforts sometimes run headlong into enormous conflicts over professional beliefs and practices that can impede progress (Achinstein, 2002). Thus even the best planned professional learning endeavors occasionally yield completely unanticipated negative consequences.

If there is concern that participants may already possess the requisite knowledge and skills, some form of pre- and post-assessment may be required. Analyzing this data provides a basis for improving the content, format, and organization of professional learning programs and activities.

Level 3: Organizational Support and Change. At Level 3 the focus shifts from participants to organizational dimensions that may be vital to the success of the professional learning experience or activity. Organizational elements also can sometimes hinder or prevent success, even when the individual aspects of professional development are done right (Sparks, 1996).

Suppose, for example, that a group of secondary educators participates in a professional learning experience on aspects of cooperative learning. As part of their experience they gain an in-depth understanding of cooperative learning theory and organize a variety of classroom activities based on cooperative learning principles. Following their learning experience they implement these activities in classes where students are graded or marked "on the curve," according to their relative standing among classmates, and great importance is attached to each student's individual class rank. Organizational grading policies and practices such as these, however, make learning highly competitive and thwart the most valiant efforts to have students cooperate and help each other learn. When graded "on the curve," students must compete against each other for the few scarce rewards (high grades) dispensed by the teacher. Cooperation is discouraged since helping other students succeed lessens the helper's chance of success (Guskey, 2000b).

The lack of positive results in this case does not reflect poor training or inadequate learning on the part of the participating teachers, but rather organizational policies that are incompatible with implementation efforts. Problems at Level 3 have essentially canceled the gains made at Levels 1 and 2 (Sparks & Hirsh, 1997). That is precisely why professional learning evaluations must include data on organizational support and change.

Level 3 questions focus on the organizational characteristics and attributes necessary for success. Did the professional learning activities promote changes that were aligned with the mission of the school? Were changes at the individual level encouraged and supported at the building and district levels (Corcoran et al., 2001)? Were sufficient resources made available, including time for sharing and reflection (Colton & Langer, 2005; Langer & Colton, 1994)? Were successes recognized and shared? Issues such as these often play a large part in determining the success of any professional learning program.

Procedures for gathering data at Level 3 differ depending on the goals of the professional learning program or activity. They may involve analyzing school records, examining the minutes from follow-up meetings, and administering questionnaires that tap issues related to the organization's advocacy, support, accommodation, facilitation, and recognition of change efforts. Structured interviews with participants and school administrators also can be helpful. These data are used not only to document and improve organizational support for professional learning, but also to inform future change initiatives.

Level 4: Participants' Use of New Knowledge and Skills. At Level 4 the primary question is this: Did the new knowledge and skills that participants learn make a difference in their professional practice? The key to gathering relevant data at this level of evaluation rests in specifying clear indicators of both the degree and quality of implementation. Unlike Levels 1 and 2, these data cannot be gathered at the end of a professional learning program or activity. Enough time must pass to allow participants to adapt the new ideas and practices to their settings. And because implementation is often a gradual and uneven process, measures of progress may need to be gathered at several time intervals.

Depending on the goals of the professional learning program or activity, these data may involve questionnaires or structured interviews with participants and their school leaders. Oral or written personal reflections, or examinations of participants' journals or portfolios also might be considered. The most accurate data typically come from direct observations, either by trained observers or using digital recordings. These observations, however, should be kept as unobtrusive as possible (for examples, see Hall & Hord, 1987).

Analyzing these data provides evidence on current levels of use. It also helps professional development leaders restructure future programs and activities to facilitate better and more consistent implementation.

Level 5: Student Learning Outcomes. Level 5 addresses "the bottom line" in education: What was the impact on students? Did the professional learning program or activity benefit them in any way? The particular student learning outcomes of interest will depend, of course, on the goals of that specific professional learning endeavor. In addition to the stated goals, the program or activity may result in important unintended outcomes. Suppose, for example, that students' average scores on large-scale assessments went up, but so did the school dropout rate. Mixed results such as this are typical in education improvement efforts and reiterate the importance of including multiple measures of student learning in all evaluations (Chester, 2005; Guskey, 2007b).

Furthermore, since stakeholders vary in their trust of different sources of evidence, it is unlikely that any single indicator of success will prove adequate or sufficient to all. For this reason, providing acceptable data for judging the effects of professional learning activities should always include multiple sources of evidence. In addition, these sources of data must be carefully matched to the needs and perceptions of different stakeholder groups (Guskey, 2012).

Results from large-scale assessments and nationally normed standardized exams may be important for accountability purposes and will need to be included. In addition, school leaders often consider these measures to be valid indicators of success. Teachers, however, generally see limitations in large-scale assessment results. These types of assessments are typically administered only once per year, and results may not be available until several months later. By that time, the school year may have ended and students promoted to another teacher's class. So while important, many teachers do not find such results particularly useful (Guskey, 2007b).

Teachers put more trust in results from their own assessments of student learning—classroom assessments, common formative assessments, and portfolios of student work. They turn to these sources of evidence for feedback to determine if the new strategies or practices they are implementing really make a difference. Classroom assessments provide timely, targeted, and instructionally relevant information that also can be used to plan revisions when needed. Since teachers comprise a major stakeholder group in any professional learning activity, sources of evidence that they trust and believe will be particularly important to include.

Measures of student learning typically include cognitive indicators of student performance and achievement, such as assessment results, portfolio evaluations, marks or grades, and scores from standardized tests. But in addition, affective and psychomotor or behavioral indicators of student performance can be relevant as well. Student surveys designed to measure how much students like school; their perceptions of teachers, fellow students, and themselves; their sense of self-efficacy; and their confidence in new learning situations can be especially informative. Evidence on school attendance, enrollment patterns, dropout rates, class disruptions, and disciplinary actions are also important outcomes. In some areas, parents' or families' perceptions may be a vital consideration. This is especially true in initiatives that involve changes in grading practices, report cards, or other aspects of school-to-home and home-to-school communication (Epstein & Associates, 2009; Guskey, 2002c).

Meaningful Comparisons

Evaluations of professional learning that extend to Level 5 should be made as methodologically rigorous as possible. Rigor, however, does not imply that only one evaluation method or design can produce credible evidence. Although randomized designs (i.e., true experimental studies) represent the gold standard in scientific research, especially in studies of causal effects, a wide range of quasi-experimental designs can produce valid results. When evaluations are replicated with similar findings, that validity is further enhanced. One of the best ways to enhance an evaluation's methodological rigor is to plan for meaningful comparisons.

In many cases data on outcomes at Level 5 are gathered from a single school or school district in a single setting for a restricted time period. Unfortunately, from a design perspective, such data lacks both reliability and validity. Regardless of whether results are positive or not, so many alternative explanations may account for the results that most authorities would consider such outcomes dubious at best and meaningless at worst (Guskey & Yoon, 2009).

It may be, for example, that the planned professional learning endeavors did, indeed, lead to noted improvements. But maybe the improvements were the result of a change in leadership or personnel instead. Maybe the community or student population changed. Maybe changes in government policies or assessments made a difference. Maybe other simultaneously implemented interventions were responsible. The possibility that these or other extraneous factors influenced results makes it impossible to draw definitive conclusions.

The best way to counter these threats to the validity of results is to include a comparison group—another similar group of educators or schools not involved in the current activity or perhaps engaged in a different activity. Ideal comparisons involve the random assignment of students, teachers, or schools to different groups. But because that is rarely possible in most education settings, finding similar classrooms, schools, or school districts provides the next best option. In some cases involvement in a professional learning activity can be staggered so that half of the group of teachers or schools that volunteer can be randomly selected to take part initially while the others delay involvement and serve as the comparison group. In other cases comparisons can be made to "matched" classrooms, schools, or school districts that share similar characteristics related to motivation, size, and demographics.

Using comparison groups does not eliminate the effects of extraneous factors that might influence results. It simply allows planners greater confidence in attributing the results attained to the particular program or activity being considered. In addition, other investigative methods may be used to formulate important questions and develop new measures relating to professional growth (Raudenbush, 2005).

Student and school records provide the majority of data at Level 5. Results from questionnaires and structured interviews with students, parents, teachers, and administrators could be included as well. Level 5 data are used summatively to document a program or activity's overall impact. But formatively, it can help guide improvements in all aspects of professional learning, including design, implementation, and follow-up. In some cases data on student learning outcomes are used to estimate the cost-effectiveness of professional learning programs and activities, sometimes referred to as "return on investment," or "ROI evaluation" (Parry 1996; J. Phillips, 1997; Todnem & Warner, 1993).

Implications for Improvement

Three important implications stem from this model for evaluating professional learning. First, each of the five evaluation levels is important. Although evaluation at any level can be done well or poorly, the data gathered at each level provides vital information for improving the quality of professional learning programs and activities. And while each level relies on different types of information that may be gathered at different times, no level can be neglected.

Second, tracking effectiveness at one level tells little about impact at the next level. Although success at an early level may be necessary for positive results at the next higher one, it is clearly not sufficient (Cody & Guskey, 1997). Breakdowns can occur at any point along the way. Sadly, most government officials and policy makers fail to recognize the difficulties involved in moving from professional learning experiences (Level 1) to improvements in student learning (Level 5). They also tend to be unaware of the complexity of this process, as well as the time and effort required to build this connection (Guskey, 1997; Guskey & Sparks, 2004).

The third implication, and perhaps the most important, is that in planning professional learning programs and activities to impact student learning, *the order of these levels must be reversed.* In other words, education leaders must plan "backward" (Guskey, 2001a, 2001b, 2003, 2014), starting where they want to end up and then working back (Hirsh, 2012).

THE IMPORTANCE OF BACKWARD PLANNING

In backward planning, educators first decide what student learning outcomes they want to achieve and what data best reflects those outcomes (Level 5). In other words, effective planning begins with articulating specific goals in terms of student learning outcomes and determining what sources of data will confirm the achievement of those goals. Relevant data on student learning outcomes provide the foundation for evaluating professional learning and the basis for accountability. School leaders and teachers must decide, for example, if they want to improve students' reading comprehension, enhance their skills in problem solving, develop their sense of confidence in learning situations, improve their behavior in class, their persistence in school, or their collaboration with classmates. Critical analyses of data from assessments of student learning, samples of student work, and school records are especially useful in identifying these student learning goals.

Next they must determine, on the basis of pertinent research, what instructional practices and policies will most effectively and efficiently produce those outcomes (Level 4). They need to ask questions such as these: What evidence verifies that these particular practices and policies will produce the results we want? How good or reliable is that evidence? Was it gathered in contexts similar to ours? In this process, leaders must be particularly mindful of innovations that are more "opinion based" than "research based," promoted by people more concerned with "what sells" to desperate educators than with "what works" with students. Before jumping on any educational bandwagon, they must make sure that trustworthy evidence validates the chosen approach.

After that, leaders need to consider what aspects of organizational support need to be in place for those practices and policies to be implemented (Level 3). Many valuable improvement efforts fail miserably due to a lack of active participation and clear support from school leaders (Guskey, 2004). Others prove ineffective because the resources required for implementation were not provided. The lack of time, instructional materials, or necessary technology can severely impede teachers' attempts to use the new knowledge and skills acquired through a professional learning experience. A big part of planning involves ensuring that organizational elements are in place to support the desired practices and policies.

Then, leaders must decide what knowledge and skills the participating professionals must have in order to implement the prescribed practices and policies (Level 2). In other words, what must they know and be able to do to successfully adapt the innovation to their specific situation and bring about the sought-after change.

Finally, consideration turns to what set of experiences will enable participants to acquire the needed knowledge and skills (Level 1). Seminars and workshops, especially when paired with collaborative planning, structured opportunities for practice with feedback, and follow-up coaching can be a highly effective means of sharing information and expanding educators' knowledge. Action research projects, organized study groups, collegial exchange, professional learning communities, and a wide range of other activities can all be effective, depending on the specified purpose of the professional learning activity.

What makes this backward planning process so important is that the decisions made at each level profoundly affect those made at the next. For example, the particular student learning outcomes being sought influence the kinds of practices and policies that need to be implemented. Likewise, the practices and policies to be implemented influence the kinds of organizational support or change required, and so on.

The context-specific nature of this work complicates matters further. Even if school leaders and teachers agree on the student learning outcomes they want to achieve, what works best in one context with a particular community of educators and a particular group of students might not work equally well in another context with different educators and different students. This is what makes developing examples of truly universal "best practices" in professional development so difficult. What works always depends on where, when, and with whom.

Unfortunately, professional learning leaders frequently fall into the same trap in planning that teachers do when they plan their lessons. Teachers often plan in terms of what they are going to do, instead of what they want their students to know and be able to do. Similarly, those planning professional learning programs and activities often focus on what they will do (workshops, seminars, institutes, etc.) and how they will do it (study groups, action research, peer coaching, etc.). Their planning tends to be "event based" or "process based." This not only diminishes the effectiveness of their efforts, but it also makes evaluation much more difficult.

The most effective professional learning planning begins with clear specification of the students' learning outcomes to be achieved and the sources of data that best reflect those outcomes. With those goals articulated, school leaders and teachers then work backward. Not only will this make planning much more efficient, but it also provides a format for addressing the issues most crucial to evaluation. As a result, it makes evaluation a natural part of the planning process and offers a basis for accountability.

SUMMARY

As we stated at the beginning, the purpose of the *Standards for Professional Learning* is to guide educators in making thoughtful decisions about professional learning experiences that will increase "educator effectiveness and results for all students" (Learning Forward, 2011). Because accomplishing this purpose requires that those decisions be based on relevant data, the Data Standard stands as clearly the most important and most crucial of all the standards.

Many good things are done in the name of professional learning. One could argue, in fact, that no educational improvement effort has ever succeeded in the absence of high-quality professional learning for educators. Unfortunately, many rotten things also pass for professional learning. What leaders in education have not done well is provide data to document the difference between the two. The *Standards,* accompanied by new demands for accountability in professional learning, make gathering and presenting that data more crucial than ever.

Showing that professional learning makes a difference, and perhaps the most important difference, will be vital in all education improvement efforts. The key to showing that difference rests in providing clear and valid data on its effectiveness. Making the Data Standard foremost in planning professional learning will help move us in that direction.

REFERENCES

Achinstein, B. (2002). Conflict amid community: The micropolitics of teacher collaboration. *Teachers College Record, 104*(3), 421–455.

Ainsworth, L., & Viegut, D. (2006). *Common formative assessments: How to connect standards-based instruction and assessment.* Thousand Oaks, CA: Corwin.

Alliger, G. M., & Janak, E. A. (1989). Kirkpatrick's levels of training criteria: Thirty years later. *Personnel Psychology, 42*(2), 331–342.

American Educational Research Association. (2000). Position statement of the American Educational Research Association concerning high-stakes testing in preK–12 education. *Educational Researcher, 29*(8), 24–25.

American Educational Research Association, American Psychological Association, & National Council on Measurement in Education. (1999). *Standards for educational and psychological testing.* Washington, DC: American Educational Research Association.

American Federation of Teachers, National Council on Measurement in Education, & National Education Association (1990). *Standards for teacher competence in educational assessment of students.* Washington, DC: National Council on Measurement in Education. Retrieved from http://www.eric.ed.gov/PDFS/ED323186.pdf

Baker, E. L. (2003). Multiple measures: Toward tiered systems. *Educational Measurement: Issues and Practice, 22*(2), 13–17.

Barton, P. E. (2002). *Staying on course in education reform.* Princeton, NJ: Statistics & Research Division, Policy Information Center, Educational Testing Service.

Bloom, B. S., Englehart, M. D., Furst, E. J., Hill, W. H., & Krathwohl, D. R. (1956). *Taxonomy of educational objectives, Handbook 1: The cognitive domain.* New York, NY: McKay.

Brennan, R. T., Kim, J., Wenz-Gross, M., & Siperstein, G. N. (2001). The relative equitability of high-stakes testing versus teacher-assigned grades: An analysis of the Massachusetts Comprehensive Assessment System (MCAS). *Harvard Educational Review, 71*(2), 173–216.

Chester, M. D. (2003). Multiple measures and high stakes decisions: A framework for combining measures. *Educational Measurement: Issues and Practice, 22*(2), 32–41.

Chester, M. D. (2005). Making valid and consistent inferences about school effectiveness from multiple measures. *Educational Measurement: Issues and Practice, 24*(4), 40–52.

Cody, C. B., & Guskey, T. R. (1997). Professional development. In J. C. Lindle, J. M. Petrosko, & R. S. Pankratz (Eds.), *1996 Review of research on the Kentucky Education Reform Act* (pp. 191–209). Frankfort: The Kentucky Institute for Education Research.

Colton, A. B., & Langer, G. M. (2005). Looking at student work. *Educational Leadership, 62*(5), 22.

Corcoran, T., Fuhrman, S. H., & Belcher, C. L. (2001). The district role in instructional improvement. *Phi Delta Kappan, 83*(1), 78–84.

Council of Chief State School Officers (CCSSO) & National Governors Association Center for Best Practices. (2010). *Common core state standards initiative.* Washington, DC: Author. http://www.corestan dards.org/the-standards

Covey, S. R. (2004). *The 7 habits of highly effective people.* New York, NY: Free Press.

Creemers, B., & Kyriakides, L. (2010). School factors explaining achievement on cognitive and affective outcomes: Establishing a dynamic model of educational effectiveness. *Scandinavian Journal of Educational Research, 54*(3), 263–294.

Duffrin, E. (1998). Math teaching in U.S. "inch deep, mile wide." *Catalyst* (online), *10*(1), September. Retrieved from http://www.catalyst -chicago.org/arch/09–98/098toc.htm

DuFour, R. (2004, May). What is a "professional learning community"? *Educational Leadership, 61*(8), 6–11.

Elmore, R. F. (2004). The problem of stakes in performance-based accountability systems. In S. H. Fuhrman & R. F. Elmore (Eds.), *Redesigning accountability systems for education* (pp. 274–296). New York, NY: Teachers College Press.

Epstein, J. L., & Associates. (2009). *School, family, and community partnerships: Your handbook for action* (3rd ed.). Thousand Oaks, CA: Corwin.

Guskey, T. R. (1997). Research needs to link professional development and student learning. *Journal of Staff Development, 18*(2), 36–40.

Guskey, T. R. (2000a). *Evaluating professional development.* Thousand Oaks, CA: Corwin.

Guskey, T. R. (2000b). Grading policies that work against standards . . . and how to fix them. *NASSP Bulletin, 84*(620), 20–29.

Guskey, T. R. (2001a). Backward planning: An outcomes-based strategy for professional development. *Curriculum in Context, 28*(2), 18–20.

Guskey, T. R. (2001b). The backward approach. *Journal of Staff Development, 22*(3), 60.

Guskey, T. R. (2002a). Does it make a difference? Evaluating professional development. *Educational Leadership, 59*(6), 45–51.

Guskey, T. R. (2002b). Professional development and teacher change. *Teachers and Teaching: Theory and Practice, 8*(3/4), 381–391.

Guskey, T. R. (2002c). *How's my kid doing? A parents' guide to grades, marks, and report cards.* San Francisco, CA: Jossey-Bass.

Guskey, T. R. (2003). Scooping up meaningful evidence. *Journal of Staff Development, 24*(4), 27–30.

Guskey, T. R. (2004). Organize principal support for professional development. *Journal of Staff Development, 25*(3), 8.

Guskey, T. R. (2005a). Mapping the road to proficiency. *Educational Leadership, 63*(3), 32–38.

Guskey, T. R. (2005b). Taking a second look at accountability. *Journal of Staff Development, 26*(1), 10–18.

Guskey, T. R. (2007a). Leadership in the age of accountability. *Educational Horizons, 86*(1), 29–34.

Guskey, T. R. (2007b). Multiple sources of evidence: An analysis of stakeholders' perceptions of various indicators of student learning. *Educational Measurement: Issues and Practice, 26*(1), 19–27.

Guskey, T. R. (2012). The rules of evidence. *Journal of Staff Development, 33*(4), 40–43.

Guskey, T. R. (2014). Planning professional learning. *Educational Leadership, 71*(8), 10–16.

Guskey, T. R., & Anderman, E. M. (2008). Students at bat. *Educational Leadership, 66*(3), 8–14.

Guskey, T. R., & Bailey, J. M. (2001). *Developing grading and reporting systems for student learning.* Thousand Oaks, CA: Corwin.

Guskey, T. R., & Bailey, J. M. (2010). *Developing standards-based report cards.* Thousand Oaks, CA: Corwin.

Guskey, T. R., & Jung, L. A. (2013). *Answers to essential questions about standards, assessments, grading, and reporting.* Thousand Oaks, CA: Corwin.

Guskey, T. R., & Sparks, D. (2004). Linking professional development to improvements in student learning. In E. M. Guyton & J. R. Dangel (Eds.), *Teacher education yearbook XII: Research linking teacher preparation and student performance.* Dubuque, IA: Kendall/Hunt.

Guskey, T. R., & Yoon, K. S. (2009). What works in professional development? *Phi Delta Kappan, 90*(7), 495–500.

Hall, G. E., & Hord, S. M. (1987). *Change in schools: Facilitating the process.* Albany, NY: SUNY Press.

Henderson-Montero, D., Julian, M. W., & Yen, W. M. (2003). Multiple measures: Alternative design and analysis models. *Educational Measurement: Issues and Practice, 22*(2), 7–12.

Hess, F. M. (2005). Commentary: Accountability policy and scholarly research. *Educational Measurement: Issues and Practice, 24*(4), 53–57.

Hill, R. K., & DePascale, C. A. (2003). Reliability of No Child Left Behind accountability designs. *Educational Measurement: Issues and Practice, 22*(3), 12–20.

Hirsh, S. (2012). Student outcomes are the driving force behind professional learning decisions. *Journal of Staff Development, 33*(5), 72.

Holton, E. F. (1996). The flawed four-level evaluation model. *Human Resources Development Quarterly, 7*(1), 5–21.

Joint Committee on Standards for Educational Evaluation. (1994). *The program evaluation standards* (2nd ed.). Thousand Oaks, CA: Sage.

Jung, L. A., & Guskey, T. R. (2012). *Grading exceptional and struggling learners.* Thousand Oaks, CA: Corwin.

Kane, M. (2002). Validating high-stakes testing programs. *Educational Measurement: Issues and Practice, 21*(1), 31–41.

Kane, T. J., & Staiger, D. O. (2002). Volatility in school test scores: Implications for test-based accountability systems. In D. Ravitch (Ed.), *Brookings papers on education policy 2002* (pp. 235–283). Washington, DC: Brookings Institute.

Kifer, E. (2001). *Large-scale assessment: Dimensions, dilemmas, and policies.* Thousand Oaks, CA: Corwin.

Kirkpatrick, D. L. (1959). Techniques for evaluating training programs. A four-part series beginning in the November issue (Vol. 13, No. 11) of *Training and Development Journal* (then titled *Journal for the American Society of Training Directors*).

Kirkpatrick, D. L. (1998). *Evaluating training programs: The four levels* (2nd ed.). San Francisco, CA: Berrett-Koehler Publishers.

Knuver, A. W. M., & Brandsma, H. (1993). Cognitive and affective outcomes in school effectiveness research. *School Effectiveness and School Improvement,* (3), 189–204.

Koretz, D. (2003). Using multiple measures to address perverse incentives and score inflation. *Educational Measurement: Issues and Practice, 22*(2), 18–26.

Krathwohl, D. R., Bloom, B. S., & Masia, B. B. (1964). *Taxonomy of educational objectives, Handbook 2: The affective domain.* New York, NY: McKay.

Lane, S., Parke, C. S., & Stone, C. A. (1998). A framework for evaluating the consequences of assessment programs. *Educational Measurement: Issues and Practice, 17*(2), 24–28.

Lane, S., & Stone, C. A. (2002). Strategies for examining the consequences of assessment and accountability programs. *Educational Measurement: Issues and Practice, 21*(1), 23–30.

Langer, G. M., & Colton, A. B. (1994). Reflective decision making: The cornerstone of school reform. *Journal of Staff Development, 15*(1), 2–7.

Larson, L. C., & Miller, T. N. (2011). 21st century skills: Prepare students for the future. *Kappa Delta Pi Record, 47*(3), 121–123.

Learning Forward. (2011). *Standards for professional learning.* Oxford, OH: Author. Retrieved from http://learningforward.org/standards#.UdsrG222o4k

Linn, R. L. (2000). Assessments and accountability. *Educational Researcher, 29*(1), 4–16.

Linn, R. L. (2003). Accountability: Responsibility and reasonable expectations. *Educational Researcher, 32*(7), 3–13.

Linn, R. L. (2005, Summer). *Fixing the NCLB accountability system* (CRESST Policy Brief 8). Los Angeles, CA: Center for Research on Evaluation, Standards, and Student Learning.

Little, J. W. (1990). The persistence of privacy: Autonomy and initiative in teachers' professional relations. *Teachers College Record, 91*(4), 509–536.

Martineau, J. A. (2010). The validity of value-added models. *Phi Delta Kappan, 91*(7), 64–67.

McMillan, J. H. (2001). Secondary teachers' classroom assessment and grading practices. *Educational Measurement: Issues and Practice, 20*(1), 20–32.

Ministerial Council on Education, Employment, Training and Youth Affairs. (2006). *Assessing student achievement in Australia.* Canberra ACT, Australia: Author. Retrieved from http://www.mceetya.edu.au/verve/_resources/Assess_student_achievement.pdf

National Research Council. (1999). *High stakes: Testing for tracking, promotion, and graduation.* J. P. Heubert & R. M. Hauser (Eds.). Washington, DC: National Academy Press.

Nitko, A. J., & Brookhart, S. M. (2010). *Educational assessment of students* (6th ed.). Upper Saddle River, NJ: Merrill/Prentice-Hall.

Parry, S. B. (1996). Measuring training's ROI. *Training & Development, 50*(5), 72–75.

Peterson, P. E., & Hess, F. M. (2005). Johnny can read . . . in some states: Assessing the rigor of state assessment systems. *Education Next, 5*(3), 52–53.

Phillips, J. J. (1997). *Return on investment in training and performance improvement programs.* Houston, TX: Gulf Publishing Co.

Phillips, P. P. (2002). *The bottom line on ROI: Basics, benefits, & barriers to measuring training & performance improvement.* Atlanta, GA: CEP Press.

Popham, W. J. (2006). Needed: A dose of assessment literacy. *Educational Leadership, 63*(6), 84–85.

Porter, A. C., Linn, R. L., & Trimble, C. S. (2005). The effects of state decisions about NCLB adequate yearly progress targets. *Educational Measurement: Issues and Practice, 24*(4), 32–39.

Raudenbush, S. W. (2005). Learning from attempts to improve schooling: The contribution of methodological diversity. *Educational Researcher, 34*(5), 25–31.

Russell, M. K., & Airasian, P. W. (2011). *Classroom assessment: Concepts and applications* (7th ed.). New York, NY: McGraw-Hill.

Schafer, W. D. (2003). A state perspective on multiple measures in school accountability. *Educational Measurement: Issues and Practice, 22*(2), 27–31.

Schmoker, M. J. (2004). Tipping point: From feckless reform to substantive instructional improvement. *Phi Delta Kappan, 85*(6), 424–432.

Schmoker, M. J. (2006). *Results now: How we can achieve unprecedented improvements in teaching and learning.* Alexandria, VA: Association for Supervision and Curriculum Development.

Scriven, M. (1991). *Evaluation thesaurus* (4th ed.). Newbury Park, CA: Sage.

Simpson, E. J. (1966). *The classification of educational objectives: Psychomotor domain.* Urbana: University of Illinois.

Sireci, S. G. (1998). Gathering and analyzing content validity data. *Educational Assessment, 5*(4), 299–321.

Sparks, D. (1996, February). Viewing reform from a systems perspective. *The Developer,* pp. 2, 6.

Sparks, D., & Hirsh, S. (1997). *A new vision for staff development.* Alexandria, VA: Association for Supervision and Curriculum Development.

Supovitz, J. A. (2002). Developing communities of instructional practice. *Teachers College Record, 104*(8), 1591–1626.

Todnem, G., & Warner, M. P. (1993). Using ROI to assess staff development efforts. *Journal of Staff Development, 14*(3), 32–34.

U.S. Congress. (2001). *No Child Left Behind Act of 2001.* Washington, DC: Author.

Weiss, M. J. (2008, March). *Examining the measures used in the federal growth model pilot program.* Paper presented at the annual meeting of the Society for Research on Educational Effectiveness, Washington, DC.

Wu, A. (1999). *The Japanese education system: A case study summary and analysis.* Washington, DC: National Institute on Student Achievement, Curriculum, and Assessment, Office of Educational Research and Improvement, U.S. Department of Education. Retrieved from http://www2.ed.gov/pubs/ResearchToday/98–3038.html

CHAPTER TWO

Using Data to Make Professional Learning Decisions

Patricia Roy

> *. . . leaders must make a fundamental shift in their focus on professional learning from how to use data systems to how to make better instructional decisions based on data contained in those systems.*
>
> Reeves & Flach, 2011, p. 40

To begin a session on effective professional development, I asked participants to create a metaphor about their learning experiences. Educators described their reactions to their professional learning with some vivid language. Some educators view professional development as a bubbling brook that gives needed sustenance and renewal. Many more consider professional learning to be more like going out on a blind date—you never know what you're getting into until you're there. It could be fun or it could be the most exasperating couple of hours you've ever spent. Others said it was like going to the dentist—it wasn't fun but you had to do it!

A recent report from TNTP (formerly The New Teacher Project) describes the survey results taken by some of the country's most highly regarded master teachers representing 36 states and 10 of the largest U.S. school districts. These master teachers rated their professional development experiences at the bottom of a list of 12 factors. The results indicate they did *not* believe that professional development helped them become better teachers or impact classroom practices (TNTP, 2013). Another large study, using data from 130,000 teachers in 50 states, found an even split—50% of teachers found value in their professional learning experiences while the other half did not (Darling-Hammond, Wei, Andree, Richardson, & Orphanos, 2009). This study also revealed that well-designed and executed professional learning is still relatively rare in the United States. Given the high expectations that the Common Core sets for teachers and their students, these results serve as one more indicator that professional learning structures and processes need to be transformed.

Standards for Professional Learning, developed by Learning Forward in collaboration with 20 national educational associations, describe seven conditions, factors, and attributes required for effective professional learning (Learning Forward, 2011). This volume in the series focuses on the use of data.

What role does data play within a high-quality professional learning system? According to Learning Forward's Data standard, there are many important uses of data when making professional learning decisions. Most essential to the process, data are collected and analyzed (1) to determine student needs and corresponding educator needs, (2) to assess teachers' progress relating to implementation of new classroom practices, and (3) to evaluate professional learning to determine its impact on teacher practice and student learning.

It might be helpful to stop for a moment and reflect on your current use of data and its use within your professional learning system. How does your school currently use data to make professional learning decisions? How are faculty members involved in the process? Do PLCs use student data to make decisions about the focus of their learning? Use the following questions to reflect on your current use of a variety of data needed to make professional learning more effective. Throughout the following sections, you will be invited to examine your current use of data in light of the information provided.

1. How do faculty members currently analyze data to determine school, educator, and student learning goals? What kinds of data do faculty members analyze? (*achievement, process, demographic, and perceptional*)
2. How often do faculty members analyze school, team, and classroom data to identify student strengths and weaknesses?
3. How are faculty members engaged in analyzing school and team data to set annual goals for student growth *and* teacher learning?
4. How are faculty members involved in the analysis of school and team data to measure progress toward annual goals for teacher learning *and* implementation of new practices?
5. How are faculty members engaged in analyzing school, team, and classroom data to make ongoing adjustments in professional learning strategies to attain desired goals?

For decades, the needs assessment survey was a primary source for determining the focus of professional learning. Its use was a result of federal and state regulations that required a needs assessment as the first step in the improvement process. A basic problem is that there seems to be a misunderstanding of the word "needs." For many years that word has been synonymous with *wants, desires, or wishes* rather than **necessities** or **requirements.** The ubiquitous needs assessment survey, while not easy to design and administer, usually consists of lists of topics, programs, or strategies from which teachers are asked to indicate what they would **like** to focus on during their professional development time. Not only are these surveys not clearly connected to student or teacher learning needs, most faculty members can complete them in less than a minute and rarely seem to remember them past the moment they hand them in. Yet, school and district professional development committees faithfully create catalogues and workshop sessions based on the survey results. Educators, on the receiving end, wonder later, "Why are we doing this topic today—what were they thinking?"

Instead of this dartboard approach, the principal, school leadership team, and learning community members need to collect, analyze, and interpret multiple sources of school data to determine individual, team, and school professional learning needs. The idea of using multiple sources of data is discussed in the second section of Guskey's beginning chapter. Because education is such a complex endeavor with many factors influencing outcomes, a single piece of data cannot reflect the whole picture nor help us pinpoint critical actions required for our improvement efforts. Multiple sources of data help us identify trends not anomalies, critical elements not momentary occurrences, and long-term remedies not short-term temporary fixes.

To clarify the connection between professional learning and improved student learning, Learning Forward provides a graphic organizer to explain that relationship in the introduction to the professional learning standards (Learning Forward, 2011, p. 16). Figure 2.1 is the graphic used to illustrate the key factors and relationships.

Figure 2.1   Relationship Between Professional Learning and Student Results

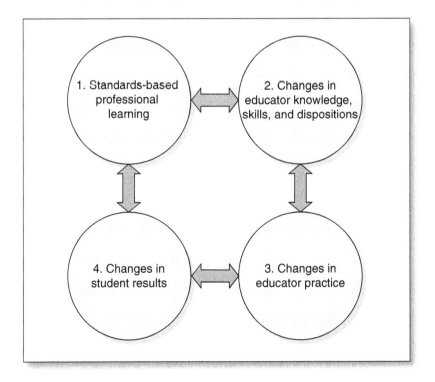

1. Effective professional learning, which is based on the standards of effectiveness and results, begins the process. Effective professional learning uses the cycle of continuous

improvement, which begins with data analysis and moves through to implementation and evaluation of results. This kind of professional learning has greater potential to change educators' classroom practices, knowledge, and beliefs.

The first action taken within an effective professional learning system is the collection and analysis of multiple forms of student learning data including interim assessments, student work, state assessments results, daily classroom work, and classroom assessments. This deep analysis of student learning needs helps focus professional learning on the topics and challenges that will make the most difference to student learning. Educator learning needs arise from student learning needs. If students are performing poorly on a science lesson, educators need to identify whether there might be a gap in their own content knowledge or whether the instructional strategies used did not facilitate the learning process. Establishing the connection between student learning needs and educator learning needs is a critical component of the process.

2. Changes in educators' knowledge, skills, and dispositions are the focus of professional learning. To determine what educators need to know and do, another set of educator and system data should be analyzed. Educator data might include information about past professional learning topics, teacher demographics, disaggregated classroom result, teacher perception, and motivation. Do content knowledge, instructional practices, assessment procedures, or a combination of factors needed to be addressed to improve student learning in targeted areas?

3. Knowledge and skills are transformed into a broader repertoire of effective instructional strategies and practices used in the classroom to assist students to improve learning and outcomes. Monitoring data are used at this step in the cycle to ensure educators understand the critical attributes of new practices and are provided feedback from skilled coaches and colleagues to support them in making the transition from knowing about strategies to actually implementing them in the classroom.

4. Finally, as a result of the use of new content knowledge and classroom practices, student learning improves. Data also play an important role at this point. Data are collected to evaluate teacher professional learning outcomes to verify that new practices are being used with quality in the classroom. When the use of new practices has been verified, then student data are collected to determine whether there are gains in student learning. The mere existence of improved student learning does not confirm that professional learning has been the primary factor in the change.

Let's contrast this process with an alternative yet common routine in many schools around the country. In this process, four days are set aside within the school calendar for professional learning. There are a variety of "programs" that the school or district has decided to adopt to improve student performance. Most teachers have not been involved in studying these new programs and are not told how they are intended to correct current practices to improve student learning. District and/or school administrators made the decision to adopt and didn't feel staff had the time or need to understand why this program was the best of many alternatives available.

Early in the year, a large group session is scheduled featuring an outside expert to explain the components of a new program. The expert wants to provide the big picture and show the many resources available to teachers when using the program. Teachers are still wondering *why* this program was chosen and what it has to do with them and their students. They are not told what they will be doing merely that there are a lot of materials available. Their attention drifts to more immediate issues typical for the start of school.

A few months later, another session is scheduled and teachers meet in small same-grade level groupings. They are asked to develop a lesson using the available materials and structure the lesson using an inquiry approach. A video is provided to demonstrate an inquiry lesson, although the students in the video are fourth graders. This single demonstration doesn't match the content or grade level for all these small working groups. Those teachers who have been using an inquiry science program steam along and complete the task. Other educators are quite lost and still don't see the connection between this new program and their student needs.

By the third session, some educators have brought student homework to correct or grade books to calculate. The majority of educators are still trying to pay attention and complete the expected tasks, but there is a growing desire to slow down the process and demand someone tell them why this new program is being adopted. With all the other new programs waiting in the wings, it has been hard to give much attention to this program except during professional development days.

Here is a major difference between the two examples: When teachers are involved in analyzing their own student data to determine learning needs and when teachers are also involved in determining what they need to know and be able to do, their reaction to and involvement in professional learning will be more focused, directed, and significant. Adults, it has been shown, are more likely to engage in learning when it solves one of their problems or challenges. Adult learners need to understand the rationale for the use of new practices and see a direct connection between those practices and student learning. Adopting the cycle provided by Learning Forward in Figure 2.1 is more likely to result in more educators understanding student learning needs as well as educator learning needs.

Another major difference is that educators, in standards-based professional learning, are involved in the decision-making process. That involvement requires the development of a new set of skills: how to analyze data to identify trends, patterns, and implications. It requires educators being able to go beyond the identification of minute, discrete annual learning issues to identifying root causes for the student learning need. For example, this year's fifth-grade male students might need to improve explanatory writing, yet the underlying cause might be organization or word choice. Many times a low achievement score in a specific area by a specific subset of students is merely a symptom of an underlying issue. When we can identify and address the underlying issue, we may correct that small issue and many other issues as well. Later in the chapter a process for uncovering root causes is explained.

ANALYZE STUDENT, EDUCATOR, AND SYSTEM DATA

Most people want to grow, they want to do better, they want to take pride in their work, but they need targets to shoot for. Unless they have clearly defined goals, the "path of least resistance" will almost always raise its ugly head.

Anderson & Feltenstein, 2007

Establishing clear educator goals begins with a deep analysis of student learning needs. This decision involves five components: (1) identifying student learning needs, (2) creating Data Summary statements, (3) analyzing root causes, (4) identifying educator learning needs, and (5) involving educators in the process. Each of these components will be described in more depth in the following section.

Identify Student Learning Needs

Educators have become accustomed to analyzing achievement data to identify and remediate student learning needs. They might be less familiar (and less comfortable) with analyzing educator data to identify their own learning needs corresponding to student needs. First, educators need to identify student learning needs and consequently determine what educators need to know and be able to do to correct those student needs.

Mentioned earlier, rather than using a single piece of achievement data—such as the state's assessment results—educators need to use multiple data sets such as formal and informal assessments; annual, benchmark, end-of-course assessments; daily classroom work; and classroom assessments. Disaggregating this data also helps pinpoint whether there is a pervasive issue or a challenge for a particular subset of students.

The following questions (Killion & Roy, 2009) can be used to focus the analysis of data by small teams of educators or learning communities. It is important to go beyond highlighting only student needs and also identify areas of strength.

- What learning do these data focus on?
- What learning objectives are being measured in each assessment?
- Which students are assessed?
- What areas of student performance are meeting or exceeding expectations?
- What areas of student performance are below expectations?
- Do patterns exist in the data?
- How did various populations of students perform? (Consider factors such as gender, race, and socioeconomic status.)
- What are other data telling us about student performance?
- How are the data similar or different in various grade levels, content areas, and individual classes?
- Where there any results that surprised us?
- What data confirms what we already know?

Educators in an elementary school in Washington state describe a process called a Data Walk, which allows the whole faculty "time to study student data, discuss it with their colleagues, and consider implications for the school and classroom" (Bergman, 2012, p. 46).

1. The process begins with the creation of charts that display reading and math achievement results for each grade level that have been posted around a room large enough to hold the faculty. The charts have been enlarged to poster size so they are easy to read and don't require each member to have their own copy.

2. Small groups of 4–5 people are formed. It is helpful to create these teams ahead of time to ensure heterogeneous membership: broad representation from different grade levels, levels of experience, special areas, and paraprofessionals. The group also has a set of sticky notes.

3. Each team stands next to a poster and discusses two questions:

   - What "ahas" do you notice from these data?
   - What questions do you have about the data?

4. After 7–10 minutes the Timekeeper calls time and each team writes at least one "aha" and one question on the sticky notes and leaves them with the data chart. Then, all teams in unison rotate to the next poster and continue the same process.

5. This rotation continues until each team has analyzed and discussed all posters.

6. When this process is completed, new groups are formed that represent same-grade level teams, with specialists divided among those teams. Each group assigns someone to serve as a recorder. Then, for 12–15 minutes each group reviews the comments and questions from its own grade-level poster(s) and discusses the implications for the grade level and the school. The recorder takes notes on these implications on a piece of large, blank poster paper.

7. After the group reconvenes, each Recorder posts the implications and reviews them in front of the whole group.

8. The whole group then discusses this question: *What did we learn as a school about the strengths and needs of our students from today's Data Walk?*

The value of doing a whole school Data Walk helps individual teachers or grade levels to identify a priority need within the school as well as differences and similarities among grade levels. This analysis and discussion also contributes to a sense of collective responsibility among staff.

Create Data Summary Statements

It is important that teams, as well as the whole faculty, identify and agree on student needs before moving into the solution phase. Data summaries require staff to examine data and describe what the data reveal by merely stating the facts—what do the data indicate—rather than jumping to a solution or assigning blame. Here's the difference: The data, for example, may indicate that in mathematics there are twice as many African American students in the needs improvement level than Caucasian students. Yet, some people will want to make a suggestion that a new mathematics program be adopted because of low scores. The first step in most problem-solving protocols is to agree *first* on the problem and then later suggest and debate possible solutions. This is a difficult discipline to maintain when interpreting data but an important skill to adopt and use (Richardson, 2000). See Figure 2.2 for examples and non-examples of data summary statements.

Data summary statements become the foundation for writing student learning goals in a SMART goal format. A SMART goal is **S**pecific, **M**easurable, **A**ttainable, **R**esults-oriented, and **T**ime-bound. (*See the Professional Learning Communities volume in this series for more information on SMART goals.*)

Analyze Root Causes

When the "facts" are clear concerning student learning needs, then a discussion of root causes comes next. This also is a necessary step in problem solving, although not a typical one. There are many root cause protocols, such as the Fishbone or Cause-Effect Diagram

Figure 2.2   Data Summary Statements: Examples and Non-examples

Example: Statement of Fact	Non-Example: Solution
Over the last three years, male students have improved 20% on the reading benchmark assessment and female students have improved 35%.	We need a pull-out program for boys in reading.
High SES students make up 85% of the top two levels in mathematics achievement on the state assessment.	Our disadvantaged students just can't handle this new mathematics; we need a remedial course for them right away.
Fifteen percent of our students mastered argumentative writing that demonstrated coherence, support for claims, and rationale for counter-claims.	How are they teaching writing in middle school? They aren't preparing our students to write argumentative tasks.

or Go for the Green (Holcomb, 1999). A seemingly simple protocol to get at root causes is called the 5 Whys (Interaction Associates, 1992, pp. 6–18). This process begins with the data summary statement that describes a student learning need. Then, the small group asks and answers the question "why" five times to identify the root cause of the define problem. Sometimes it might take more than five questions and sometimes it might take less. See Figure 2.3 for an example of the 5 Whys Protocol.

This process might have concluded after the number 4 answer. Educators might not know why ELL students are less involved during small group learning, which might require them to survey students or to do some observation of student learning groups to identify the reasons or to examine educational research. They could have found Elizabeth Cohen's work on status expectation, a component of Complex Instruction (Cohen, 1994). This work suggests that status in groups can be altered and managed by the teacher through helping students understand how to work within a group as well as redesigning curriculum materials to include more visual cues so that students do not have to know how to read to be involved in classroom and small group work. The 5 Whys digs deep into identifying causes which may result in a different type of solution. When confronted

Figure 2.3   Example of the 5 Whys Protocol

Data Summary Statement: There is a 30% gap between ELL students and non-ELL students in the functions and algebraic thinking area of mathematics.

Q1: Why is there a 30% gap between ELL and non-ELL students in functions and algebraic thinking?

A1: This area falls within the expressions and equations domain and has much more rigorous expectations than we have had before in middle school.

Q2: Why are ELL students having more difficulty with these rigorous expectations?

A2: They are having difficulty understanding the concepts and applying them in practice.

Q3: Why are ELL students having a difficult time understanding concepts and applying them?

A3: They are not as engaged during small group learning activities that have focused on these areas.

Q4: Why are ELL students not as engaged during small group learning activities?

A4: Non-ELL students take over the manipulatives and don't ask the ELL students to participate.

Q5: Why do non-ELL students dominate the small group work?

A5: They have higher status within the group and don't believe the ELL students have anything to contribute.

Q6: Why do ELL students have less status within the small groups?

A6: ELL students have less status in the classroom as well.

with a similar finding, many schools might have sent ELL students to a computer program to learn more about mathematics' functions and algebraic thinking.

Identify Educator Learning Needs

The final step in this process is to identify educator learning needs that correspond to and align with student learning needs. There are a number of questions to consider when making decisions about educator needs.

1. What content knowledge may educators need to develop to improve student learning results?

2. Which instructional practices need to be developed or refined to address student learning needs? Is there research or best practice that identifies instructional practices for this area of need?

3. What assessment strategies need to be developed or refined to improve student learning results?

4. What combination of knowledge, instruction, and assessment factors may need to be addressed to resolve student learning needs?

Once these questions have been answered, then educator learning goals are established. One format that is helpful in pinpointing educator learning needs is called KASAB: an acronym that stands for **K**nowledge, **A**ttitudes, **S**kills, **A**spirations, and **B**ehaviors. KASAB can help break down educator learning goals into finer, discrete, grain-size goals and focus on the knowledge needed to be understood, skills needed to be developed, and behaviors needed to be used (Killion, 2008). More detail on the definition and examples of KASAB can be found in the Professional Learning Communities volume of this series.

Educator learning goals are also established and written in a SMART goal format. SMART goals establish specific results or outcomes as well as evidence that will demonstrate that the outcome has been accomplished and a timeline for reaching the expected result. To demonstrate the relationship between educator learning goals and student learning needs, the two can be combined. For example,

- By the fall of next school year, middle school mathematics teachers will learn and consistently implement status expectation strategies with quality as measured by the Complex

Instruction Observation Tool. The results will be a 12% reduction between ELL students and non-ELL students in functions and algebraic thinking as measured by the district benchmark assessment.

- In three years, 90% of third-grade students will read on grade level as a result of teachers learning and implementing with quality new instructional strategies for word decoding (Munger, 2010, p. 40).

Involve Educators in the Process

Involving the faculty in these discussions, dialogues, and debates is important. But this might first require building their data analysis skills so that they are comfortable, competent, and confident in analyzing achievement data as well as other forms of student and educator data. Earlier it was argued that educator involvement would lead to ownership and commitment to change. Their involvement also builds collective responsibility for student learning. Collective responsibility is a value that exists within some schools when educators are jointly committed to the success of all students who attend the school, work together to ensure the success of every teacher, and work collaboratively to build each teacher's expertise and competence. Collective responsibility builds a collaborative culture within the building, which has been recognized as an important component of an effective school.

ASSESSING PROGRESS

> . . . the three keys to inspiring change . . . **reinforce, reinforce, reinforce.** Many leaders in times of change grossly underestimate the need for continuous reinforcement. During a time of change, we have doubts, fears, and occasional disappointments. The challenge is how do you keep the change alive until the behavior is consistent with your goals?
>
> Anderson & Feltenstein, 2007

Educators have learned to create and use formative assessments of student learning to monitor progress toward an ultimate student learning outcome. Yet, many schools are not currently gathering formative data on educator practice to monitor their use of new instructional and curricular practices. These data are not used to evaluate educators but to determine whether benchmarks are appropriate, provide additional assistance and support, or make adjustments to professional learning designs and strategies to increase educator learning and implementation. Assessing progress produces a juncture at which professional learning and the process of change intersect.

Monitoring assists us in supporting educators as they make a change in their daily classroom practice. Our culture is steeped in adages about the difficulty of change: *The only people who like change are babies with wet diapers,* or *this change may be the answer to my prayers but it's not the answer I was praying for.* The critical need for assessing progress is based on work in the many areas of change. The difficulty of changing daily habits and work behavior is part of the human condition, whether in schools or other lines of business. Jeffrey Pfeffer and Robert Sutton (2000) explain the phenomenon of the knowing-doing gap: where knowledge replaces actual changes in behavior. The authors explain that many organizations, including educational systems, build their workers' knowledge but never assist and support those same employees to make the transition of actually putting that knowledge to work. They found that leadership talks a great game and uses all the buzz words, but a quick observation of how employees are working or interacting shows very little change in daily practice.

What are some of the processes and procedures that can help educators transfer knowledge into practice? How can we support and assist educators as they learn about new practices and then actually implement them in their classrooms? This is an essential component of effective professional learning: educators' use of new classroom strategies leads to improved student learning. Among those processes recognized by research and good practice are (1) establishing benchmarks, (2) defining what the new practice looks like in operation, and (3) monitoring educators' classroom practices. Each of these processes will be described in the next section.

Establish Benchmarks of Progress

Many educators still think of professional learning as a simple action-reaction relationship: new knowledge leads inevitably to changes in classroom practices—*X* causes *Y*. A more realistic metaphor for the change process might be that professional learning is like a cross-country journey—a journey without the use of a GPS that probably also includes lots of detours, traffic snarls, and construction zones. At a minimum, we would want to know key destinations along the way where we could check in to make sure we were on the right track. Those key destinations or benchmarks would allow us to make some minor course corrections early in the process rather than waiting to find out we made the wrong turn in Kankakee and are now wildly off course, states away from where we wanted to go. What most of us really want is our GPS to show restaurants, hotels, rest stops, construction zones, and alternative routes.

Many of the changes in practice we ask educators to make never provide detailed maps and are filled with many detours and construction zones. Educators also need checkpoints along the way to determine whether they are on course. Benchmarks allow them to determine whether they are on track or need to make small or large course corrections as well.

When Rosabeth Moss Kanter, world renowned for her applied work in organization change, focused on school improvement work, she identified building a public, transparent system for monitoring progress of the use of new practices as an essential leadership practice. Her recommendations about a monitoring system include

- identifying clear and discrete benchmarks—events or results that illustrate an incremental step toward the desired outcome;
- sharing benchmarks publicly so that staff can monitor their own progress;
- using a wide variety of measures of progress;
- adjusting intermediate goals and benchmarks based on data;
- creating systems that allow identification of both successes and problems and pinpoint where support might be needed;
- celebrating when progress has been made; and
- sharing this monitoring information across the system (Kanter, n.d.).

We need to monitor the effectiveness of professional learning by continuously collecting data on whether the plan has accomplished our intended outcomes and results for educators. Creating a monitoring and benchmark system may seem an overwhelming task, but a tool called the 30–60–90, developed by Susan Bailey (2000), is a simple way to begin creating a benchmark system.

You begin with a priority goal that you have decided should be implemented. Administrators, the school leadership team, and teachers then identify what they think they could/should accomplish in the first 30 days, then in 60 days, then in 90 days. This allows the change to be broken into smaller, bite-size pieces, and signifies to staff an area of monthly focus. Being able to implement big changes in incremental steps has been found to increase the likelihood that people will actually try the new practice. It's like the old joke: *How do you eat an elephant?* **One bite at a time.**

Because this chart (Figure 2.4) can represent a whole school or grade-level goal, it can also encourage and support peer learning and collaboration within learning teams, PLCs, or among teaching partners. Planning and accomplishing these benchmarks can and should be done collaboratively so that staff shares their ideas, practices, and strategies as well as problem-solves barriers and challenges.

Once the primary focus is identified, staff also pinpoint specific examples for the rest of the chart—what are adults doing, and so on. Notice, in the example, that the major focus remains the same for 90 days. In fact, the major focus can remain the same for an entire year, yet specific strategies and practices might change every month.

Identifying a tool or strategy that will be used also identifies what evidence or artifacts can be collected to help the school or team keep track of its progress toward accomplishing the ultimate goal of improved student reading comprehension. Staff members can be expected to bring those artifacts (student work, descriptions of lessons, copies of questions, reflections on how it went, scores from a reading assessment, etc.) to a faculty meeting where individuals or small groups share with each other what has been done and reflect on how the new strategies are making a difference for student learning. Sometimes, the focus of the staff meetings might be on problem-solving challenges to implementation. Kanter counsels us that effective monitoring systems also need to identify problems in order to solve them before they become gigantic barriers to implementation.

Periodically, progress should be celebrated. Kanter has called this part of the change process the miserable middles of change. Everything looks like a failure in the middle. In the middle, our highly energetic kick-off of a new, promising practice has hit the

Figure 2.4 Sample 30–60–90 Monitoring Chart

Elements	30 Days	60 Days	90 Days
Our major focus	Reading comprehension	Reading comprehension	Reading comprehension
What adults are doing	Focusing on developing a range of questions including higher-level thinking	Focusing on developing a range of questions including higher-level thinking	Focusing on developing a range of questions including higher-level thinking
What students are doing	Majority of time students use higher-order thinking skills	Majority of time students use higher-order thinking skills	Majority of time students use higher-order thinking skills
Skills being learned	Compare and contrast	Compare and contrast	Classifying: Organize according to similarities
Tools and materials being used	Graphic organizers: Venn Diagram	Graphic organizers: Comparison Matrix	Graphic organizers: Bubble Chart
Challenges benefits, and frustrations	Teachers and students will be frustrated because they won't feel successful at this yet	Student frustration, matching questions to those found on the state assessment	Teachers need to scaffold learning to assist special needs students with higher order—these questions are rare

doldrums of hard work, extra planning, and challenging experiments with new classroom practices. We need to take note and celebrate our growth, our movement, and our incremental improvements.

Principals have done something as simple as bringing in large bowls of popcorn and a beverage to the staff meeting. Others bring in a decorated sheet cake and sparkling apple juice to make the celebration a bit more festive. A friend who was an elementary principal decided to recognize the hard work of her staff by giving each one a simple glass vase with a single red rose to signify their hard work and dedication to student learning. Celebrations are important not only en route but when we reach goal achievement to acknowledge risk taking and the importance of taking those "small bites."

Monitoring: Classroom Observations, Rounds, and Walk-Throughs

Classroom observations, instructional rounds, and walk-throughs are useful ways to collect and monitor implementation of new classroom practices. The groundwork for effective use of these strategies is a clear and concise definition of the new practice *in operation.* These descriptions should be shared frequently and broadly with staff members so there are no surprises or "gotcha" moments as observations occur.

A useful tool for monitoring implementation of new practices is called Innovation Configuration (IC) maps. They were first developed by Gene Hall and Shirley Hord during their time at the Research and Development Center in Austin, Texas. They were first to recognize and establish that clear and explicit descriptions of new practices were missing from much of the training provided at the time. These IC descriptions defined what the new procedures entailed when put into practice in the classroom. They also found that teachers did not implement the innovation in the same way nor at the same speed. Some staff moved swiftly to adopt new classroom practices while others utilized some components of the innovation but not all of them. As a result, their IC descriptions also included identifying essential components as well as a continuum of practices, which ranged from ideal to not-yet-begun levels of implementation (Hall & Hord, 2011). Explaining how to create an Innovation Configuration map is beyond the scope of this section, but more information about developing maps will be found in the Implementation volume of this series.

Another simple tool that can be used for beginning classroom observation or monitoring is the Practice Profile (Horsley & Loucks-Horsley, 1998). The Practice Profile involves developing a precise description of what effective implementation looks like and what it doesn't look like. Six to eight essential components are identified along with descriptive examples of teacher and/or student behavior. Often these behaviors are categorized into three levels: Ideal, Acceptable, and Unacceptable. A sample Practice Profile (Figure 2.5) is provided that describes the role of the principal in collecting and analyzing data to assess progress toward professional learning goals.

Figure 2.5   Practice Profile

How closely is the principal using formative data to assess the school's progress toward professional learning benchmarks and goals?

Ideal:

- Collects formative data monthly
- Works in cooperation with the school leadership team and staff to collect and analyze data
- Focuses data on professional learning benchmarks and goals
- Analyzes formative data monthly
- Identifies progress and barriers to implementation
- Assists staff and teams to make adjustments to professional learning designs and strategies to remove barriers and improve progress

Acceptable:

- Collects formative data quarterly
- Works in cooperation with the school leadership team and staff to collect and analyze data
- Focuses data on professional learning benchmarks
- Analyzes formative data quarterly
- Makes in-process, data-based adjustments in schoolwide professional learning

Unacceptable:

- Fails to collect or analyze formative data to measure progress of professional learning goals
- Does not establish professional learning benchmarks for teacher classroom practice

The purpose of monitoring progress is to make midcourse corrections in the professional learning plan. These corrections could involve using different types of learning designs, reinforcing and building deeper knowledge of critical attributes of new practice, or providing staff time to collaboratively plan new lessons and units. It might also involve identifying staff members who seem to be making fast-paced changes and which ones are having a little more trouble launching into new activities. With that information, we could, for example, create learning teams and have them work directly with a specialist or building-level coach to build needed knowledge and skills.

Our long-term professional learning plans are based on a hypothesis and educated guesses about the amount of time staff may need to learn and use new practices. Formative data can tell us whether our timeframes and plans were realistic. If not, the data will indicate changes that need to be made in order to accomplish our goals.

A district in Kentucky collected and analyzed data on their efforts to help educators understand the Common Core standards and plan units of instruction. The formative data they collected and analyzed on a monthly basis showed that their hypothesis about the amount of time needed was wrong. The staff worked together to understand the Common Core standards and then wrote lesson plans and units. A review of those plans by curriculum specialists and other central office staff showed that educators had not fully grasped the instructional shifts demanded by the standards. Based on that data, they decided to return to the concept of the instructional shift but address the learning in a new way.

They had originally introduced the topic by providing a short lecture, a video on the topic, and some lesson examples. They decided to have staff read summaries of lessons—some lessons that made the shift while others had not. Small groups were asked to rate how well the lessons demonstrated the instructional shift and explain why they had rated them the way they did. They were asked to highlight specific examples within the lesson that were examples of the shift. Three small groups met with a specialist to review and discuss their ratings and rationales. Time to reflect on what they had learned was structured into the session, and tweets summarizing their learning were posted on a group online site.

Just as in the classroom, we need to monitor learning and adjust learning plans to meet the needs of staff. This district found that sometimes you have to go slow to go fast!

EVALUATE PROFESSIONAL LEARNING

Trust, but verify.

Russian proverb

We're probably all used to the short evaluation surveys provided at the end of a training session. It typically asks whether the presenter was organized, whether the material was useful, and whether the coffee and other refreshments were adequate. While this information is useful to gain some understanding of how participants react to an individual session, an evaluation of professional learning goes more deeply and explicitly into answering two primary questions:

1. Did teachers change their practice in the classroom and use those new practices with fidelity?

2. As a result of changes in teacher practice, did student learning improve?

These questions emerge from the model presented in Figure 2.1, which describes the relationship between professional learning and student results. Some districts overlook answering the first question when evaluating professional learning; they don't check to see whether classroom practices have changed or whether they are being performed with fidelity to the model. The linkages within the professional learning model illustrate that improved student learning *result* from the use of new practices within the classroom. A comprehensive evaluation of professional learning examines results not efforts, monitors and assesses the quality of implementation not seat time and hours spent learning, and evaluates outcomes not intentions.

Erroneously, districts sometimes only examine student achievement data at the end of the year to determine whether student learning has improved and then attribute the change *or lack of change* to professional learning. These results are then used to make decisions to abandon new programs and practices that might not yet have even been implemented in classrooms. Change research indicates, depending on how complex the new procedures are compared to what is being currently used in the classroom, that full and deep implementation of new practices by a majority of staff can take three to five years. These districts then are missing an examination of an essential link in the change process—has there been any change in classroom practices that could be correlated to student improvement? This is sometimes referred to as a Black Box evaluation (Killion, 2008). A Black Box evaluation indicates only whether student learning has changed but can't tell us *why* that outcome occurred. A Glass Box evaluation will link the input factors to results. It explains whether classroom coaching led to higher-quality implementation in the classroom, for example (see Figure 2.6).

Evaluating whether educator practice has changed requires a new set of knowledge and skills for building and district administrators, instructional coaches, and teacher leaders. Yet, the same tools and processes used to monitor progress, explained in the last section of this chapter, are also used to determine the quantity and quality of implementation of new practices. This step of the evaluation process is also described by Guskey in *Level 4: Participants' Use of New Knowledge and Skills* in the first chapter of this volume. As noted by Guskey, this information can be used to restructure professional learning to ensure more educators implement desired practices with quality, thus resulting in improved student learning.

Guskey's work, in the first part of this volume, describes one model of professional learning evaluation. Another professional learning evaluation model was developed by Joellen Killion (2008). The critical components of an evaluation framework developed by Killion are provided in Figure 2.7. These are key decisions that need to be made when planning a comprehensive evaluation of professional learning. Each of the components will be described in more detail in the next part of this section.

Figure 2.6   Black Box Evaluation and Glass Box Evaluation

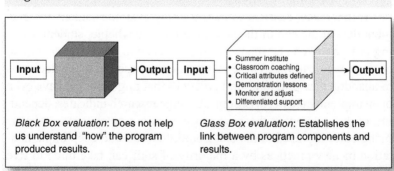

Figure 2.7 Killion's Evaluation Framework Components

Program Goals	Measurable Objectives	Information/Data Needed	Data Sources	Data Collection	Data Analysis	Time Line	Location
What does the program intend to accomplish?	What changes are anticipated for students? To what degree? What changes are anticipated for educators? To what degree?	What is the best way to determine whether the change has occurred? What information will tell us that?	What/who is the best source of information about the intended change? What is already available? What might have to be created to gather the information needed?	How will the data be collected?	How will the data be examined to determine whether change did occur? Will descriptive or inferential statistics be needed?	When will data be collected?	Where will data be collected?

Source: Killion, 2008. Copyright © 2008 Corwin. Used with permission.

Program Goals

A clear statement of the goals for the program that is being evaluated needs to be stated. What change is expected as a result of educators using the new program as intended? Will student learning increase, will student behaviors improve, will higher-level questions be answered correctly by more students—especially special education students? Will teacher classroom practices change? Is that change expected by all staff or all reading teachers? Does the goal require comparing results to earlier outcomes? More consistent student engagement in mathematics classrooms implies that there is baseline data describing the current level of student engagement.

Measurable Objectives

Measurable objectives establish clear outcomes for student learning as well as clear outcomes for teacher learning and implementation. Stating them using a SMART goal format is useful. A SMART goal is Specific, Measurable, Attainable, Results-oriented, and Time-bound. An example of a SMART goal is, "In three years, all eighth-grade students will improve 15% in the mastery level or better in mathematics functions and algebraic thinking as measured by the district's benchmark assessment."

This goal is specific because it indicates the focus is on eighth-grade students in the area of functions and algebraic thinking. It is measurable because it states evidence from the district benchmark will be used to determine whether the goal has been met. It is attainable because the result is expected within three years. It is results-oriented because it states an increase of 15% in a specific area of mathematics instruction—functions and algebraic thinking. Finally, it is time-bound because three years are allowed for this outcome to occur.

A SMART goal for educators could be, "In two years, seventh- and eighth-grade mathematics teachers will learn and consistently implement identified instructional strategies* that improve functions and algebraic thinking as measured by an Innovation Configuration map." This goal is specific because it focuses on specific instructional strategies. The asterisk would provide further information by naming and defining the strategies staff will be expected to use. It is measurable though the collection of data defined in an Innovation Configuration map. Whether it is attainable depends on a number of factors including whether and how math teachers were involved in making this decision. It is results-oriented because it sets an expectation that all mathematics teachers will implement the new strategies, and those behaviors will be observed and evidence will be collected concerning how well they are used in the classroom. The goal is time-bound because the result is expected within two years.

Information or Data Needed

When a SMART goal is written explicitly, the data is already identified. In the examples above, district benchmark assessments focused on functions and algebraic thinking will be used to determine whether the results have been accomplished. For educators, the results from observations using an Innovation Configuration map will be analyzed to determine whether teachers are using new instructional practices with quality in their classrooms.

Data Sources

Data sources include identifying specific instruments, processes for collecting data, and tools. It might also indicate whether a new tool or assessment needs to be developed. Following our example from above, the district benchmark assessment already has items that focus on functions and algebraic thinking, but additional items could be added if possible. An Innovation Configuration map for the instructional strategies would need to be developed unless the provider already has developed the tool or at least has clear descriptions of critical attributes of the practices along with specific definitions of what the practice looks like in operation.

Data Collection

This part of a comprehensive plan indicates how data will be collected including who may be involved. Again, following the example above, the district benchmark assessment includes a clear procedure for administration. Classroom data collection could include evidence gathered by building administrators, district mathematics specialists, instructional coaches, and experienced colleagues from the mathematics department in the school as well as other schools.

Data Analysis

This component of the evaluation plan indicates how the data will be analyzed. In the case of student learning data, there would be a comparison between the first or baseline district assessment results with the most current results to determine whether there was a 15% increase in the number of students who reached the mastery level.

In the case of using an Innovation Configuration map, results are usually aggregated to show the percentage of educators implementing new practices at different levels. Beginning with a baseline observation is helpful to determine the quantity and quality of change of practice.

Timeline

How much data and how frequently this data are collected would be determined in this component of the plan. Using the district benchmark schedule would already determine that timeline. For educator observation, you would have to determine whether instructional observation data will be collected monthly, biweekly, or every quarter. Creating the schedule and assignments for classroom observation and data collection would become a critical part of this component especially if it involved district personnel and educators from other schools.

Location

This component explains where the data will be collected. In the continuing example, student data are collected in the classroom through the district benchmark assessment. For educators, the data are also collected in the classroom through a structured observation using an Innovation Configuration map.

The purpose of the evaluation plan is to ensure that a comprehensive data collection system has been defined early in the process. The plan's framework details the tasks, timeline, personnel, and tools required to complete the evaluation. The plan is created before formal professional learning occurs to ensure that data are available and collected systematically. More than one district or school has found that if they wait until the *end* of a project or program to think about evaluation, they cannot go back and collect the data they need to objectively assess the program's effectiveness, merit, or worth.

Making decisions before introducing an initiative is a proactive step to ensure you have the evidence you need to show that the school or district's professional learning efforts are making a difference to students.

Use Evaluation Results to Improve Professional Learning

An important use of evaluation results is to improve professional learning strategies, learning designs, support systems, and educator results. One of the underlying assumptions of professional learning is that when educators learn and use new knowledge and strategies in the classroom, then student learning should improve. The knowledge and use of new strategies and practices should be evidence based to demonstrate that their use has made a difference in student learning or other desired outcomes.

One district's evaluation plan collected and analyzed a program to improve student engagement during instruction. One of the primary strategies was the use of small student learning teams. The teams gave students an opportunity to learn from and with each other, a significant finding from instructional research. Frequent classroom walk-throughs found that students were, in fact, spending a lot of time in small groups.

Yet, a closer look at what was actually happening within those small groups revealed something very different was occurring. High-quality student engagement was defined as all students having the opportunity to participate. Students were assigned roles, yet when observers collected data about student interaction during group time they found that some students barely participated; when they did talk, no one recognized their contributions or commented on their ideas. Further, some groups became dominated by one or two students who did all the work, did most of the talking, and handed out menial tasks to other members, such as picking up materials or cleaning up.

This finer-grained description of effective student learning groups defines high-fidelity or high-quality student learning. Merely being seated in a group setting is not what contributes to a better student learning experience; it is the quality of interaction between students that makes a difference.

In this case, the district built on the foundation that had already been established concerning the use of small learning teams and refined classroom practice by introducing the critical attributes of high-quality student learning teams: everyone doing the work together, no single team member doing all the work, students providing help to others until they could do the work, and everyone preparing to explain how the work was done.

Tool: Theory of Change

A theory of change is a helpful tool that can assist schools and districts to create a comprehensive evaluation plan including both formative and summative evaluation. A theory of change assists principals, the school leadership team, and instructional coaches to define the major components of a professional learning plan and explain the sequence of those components. It can highlight the kinds of resources that will be needed to make the change in practice (see Figure 2.8). It also illustrates how those steps lead up to and support intermediate or long-range changes in educator practices and student outcomes. A theory of change also articulates the underlying assumptions that are the foundation of the plan and makes explicit the thinking that undergirds the plan. For example, do the planners believe that classroom coaching is imperative for effective implementation of new strategies or that educators will use new strategies when mandated to do so?

This theory of change is based on the following underlying assumptions:

- When teachers understand various instructional strategies and have time to plan lessons and gather materials, they can be expected to use them.
- In order to use new instructional strategies, teachers need to have the appropriate resources.
- Successful use of new strategies builds with increased practice and support.
- Classroom-based coaching and teacher collaboration is the best way to support teachers as they apply new practices.
- Consistent use of new practices comes over time.
- Student achievement results from consistently applied practices delivered by teachers who have in-depth understanding of content and content-specific instructional strategies.

Figure 2.8   Sample Theory of Change of Improving Achievement of Below-Level Students

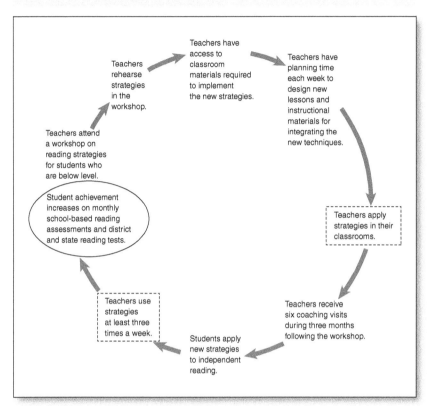

Source: Adapted from Killion, 2008, p. 57. Copyright © 2008 Corwin. Adapted with permission.

In this theory of change, before teachers are expected to use new reading strategies in the classroom, four activities occur: (1) a formal workshop in which educators learn about new reading strategies for below-level student readers, (2) time to practice new strategies is provided within the workshop and constructive feedback provided, (3) teachers are provided access to classroom materials required for the new strategies, and (4) teachers have collaborative planning time to design lessons and integrate new materials used with the new techniques. The first three underlying assumptions support this sequence of activities; these assumptions are also grounded in research on professional learning and change.

A benchmark or interim outcome needed to accomplish the long-term outcome of improved student learning is that teachers are able to apply the new strategies in their classroom (boxed items in Figure 2.8). The evaluation plan might include collecting data to show that teachers are using new strategies and that time for planning preceded that interim goal. Another appropriate goal would be to clearly define what quality implementation of the new strategies looks like in practice. That description becomes the basis for classroom observation of the strategies; it might also include a requirement that teachers create a log that shows when they have used the strategies during instruction so that those logs could be reviewed to determine whether the strategies are being used at least three times a week during reading instruction.

The theory of change can also be used as a preventive measure to check the components of the learning plan against evidence-based professional learning practices to identify other components that may need to be added. For example, a single workshop, the first step of the theory of change, may not allow enough detailed information about the new reading strategies for every teacher. An additional component would be a quick diagnosis of teacher lesson plans and inclusion of a follow-up mini-session to review critical attributes so that everyone has a common understanding of the new strategies.

CONCLUSION

Data play an essential role in making professional learning decisions. It creates focus—attention to priority student learning needs and corresponding educator learning needs. Involving staff in authentic analysis and interpretation is essential because it builds an understanding of why new practices are needed and how some classroom challenges can be addressed. Data sometimes serve as "the canary in the coal mine," pointing out areas of need that cause us to delve more deeply into the issues to find the underlying source of persistent student learning challenges.

Data are the foundation of effective monitoring systems. Continuous assessment of progress toward a desired outcome helps educators make midcourse corrections to avert small detours, find their way around roadblocks, and recalculate to get us back to the quickest route to our final destination—improved student learning.

Monitoring also points out whether or not we have reached intermediate goals, which also reminds us to stop, celebrate, and relish our progress.

Data facilitate systematic evaluation of results. Professional learning evaluation focuses on implementation of new strategies, not just learning about them. Professional learning evaluation focuses on impact, not merely on effort or seat time required to learn. Professional learning evaluation focuses on outcomes for teachers and their students, not merely intentions or hope.

Data also serve additional purposes in schools and districts:

1. To illustrate to staff how their efforts to learn new strategies and practices pays off in improved student learning. So many schools and districts adopt many more initiatives than they can possibly implement with high quality. The result, for many teachers, is that they are working very diligently on a multitude of innovations but don't have enough time to learn them deeply or implement them with quality. This can lead to an unintended consequence: They are working hard on new programs yet don't see changes in student learning. They can begin to believe that nothing will make a difference for their students and begin to doubt any new idea or practice will make a difference. They need to see when they work together and support each other's use of new classroom practices that their efforts will result in improved student learning. Data can link efforts to those results.

2. To demonstrate the relationship between professional learning and student learning. There are times when system administrators, school board members, parents, and other community members don't understand why time needs to be provided, within the schedule, for educators to learn together and collaborate. They may not understand why educators don't already know what they need to know or only view PLC time as an inconvenience or a child care challenge. Data collected throughout the process can inform the school's constituents about needs, progress, and results of professional learning efforts and activities.

3. To inform school staff and the leadership team about how staff members react to and participate in the change process.

Most schools have staff who might love to learn with small learning teams yet have a small number of teachers who truly work better independently. There will be some educators who relish sharing their lessons and units with colleagues while others feel intimidated by that prospect. There are some staff who will never request coaching while others will have a few trusted colleagues who provide guidance, engage in problem solving, and celebrate progress. This information is important when designing professional learning and supporting staff to make continuous improvement to their practice.

REFERENCES

Anderson, M., & Feltenstein, T. (2007). *Change is good . . . you go first.* Naperville, IL: Simple Truths.

Bailey, S. (2000). *Making progress visible: Implementing standards and other large scale change initiatives.* Vacaville, CA: Bailey Alliance Inc.

Bergman, B. (2012, August). Put data in the driver's seat: A deeper understanding of achievement results in leading change in one Washington district. *Journal of Staff Development, 33*(4), 44–47.

Cohen, E. (1994). *Designing groupwork: Strategies for the heterogeneous classroom.* New York, NY: Teacher College Press.

Darling-Hammond, L., Wei, R. C., Andree, A., Richardson, N., and Orphanos, S. (2009, February). Professional learning in the learning profession: A status report on teacher development in the United States and abroad. Oxford, OH: National Staff Development Council and The School Redesign Network at Stanford University.

Hall, G., & Hord, S. (2011). *Implementing change: Patterns, principles, and potholes* (3rd ed.). Boston, MA: Allyn & Bacon.

Holcomb, E. (1999). *Getting excited about data: How to combine people, passion, and proof.* Thousand Oaks, CA: Corwin.

Horsley, D., & Loucks-Horsley, S. (1998, Fall). CBAM brings order to the tornado of change. *Journal of Staff Development,* 19(4), 17–20.

Interaction Associates. (1992). *Collaborative problem solving.* San Francisco, CA: Author.

Kanter, R. M. (n.d.). *Are our change measures and milestones adequate?* http://www.reinventingeducation.org

Killion, J. (2008). *Assessing impact: Evaluating staff development* (2nd ed.). Thousand Oaks, CA: Corwin & NSDC.

Killion, J., and Roy, P. (2009). *Becoming a learning school.* Oxford, OH: National Staff Development Council.

Learning Forward. (2011). *Standards for professional learning.* Oxford, OH: Author. Retrieved from http://learningforward.org/standards#.Ud srG222o4k

Munger, L. (2010). *Change, lead, succeed: Building capacity with school leadership teams.* Oxford, OH: Learning Forward.

Pfeffer, J., & Sutton, R. (2000). *The knowing-doing gap: How smart companies turn knowledge into action.* Boston, MA: Harvard Business School Press.

Reeves, D., & Flach, T. (2011, August). Data: Meaningful analysis can rescue schools from drowning in data. *Journal of Staff Development, 32*(4), 34–40.

Richardson, J. (2000, October/November). The numbers game: Measure progress by analyzing data. *Tools for Schools,* p. 4.

TNTP. (2013, August 13). *Perspectives of irreplaceable teachers: What America's best teachers think about teaching.* http://tntp.org/ideas-and -innovations/view/perspectives-of-irreplaceable-teachers

Chapter Three

The Case Study

Valerie von Frank

Most readers of this case study will find a district that is different from theirs. The temptation is to say this district is too rich or more disadvantaged, larger or smaller, more urban, more rural, more or less diverse. Doing so misses the value of a case study.

The questions at the heart of the matter are about how well this system stands up when we consider the major strands of this specific standard for professional learning. In reading the case study, it's fair to ask how the system meets the individual standard, as well as in what ways it may not. It's helpful to consider how well the district meets the other standards for professional learning, which top-performing systems generally do because of the interconnected nature of the standards. Most effective systems working to achieve one standard strive toward quality professional learning that meets multiple standards. But in the real world, as they reach, they also may fall short in one area or another.

The decision for this series to use real, journalistic-style rather than fictionalized case studies was deliberate. The intent is for readers to hear educators' voices from actual practice, to see examples of what is possible and what it looks like to work to the level of a specific standard for professional learning—including some aspects that may not fully exemplify the standard. The districts were chosen based on research, interviews, and solid evidence that student outcomes are improving, because student achievement is the ultimate goal of professional learning. Professional learning does not take place for its own sake, but to enable teachers to teach effectively so that every student achieves.

Often these days it seems we are tempted to focus on our differences rather than seeking the good we can find in the model before us. Reading a case study should invite that certain amount of critique, but also of recognition if not admiration. Rather than losing the point by focusing on differences and perceived shortcomings, we invite you to consider the standard at hand. Review its main components. Ask how this district exemplifies those elements. Listen carefully to what those at each level of the system said about learning from their vantage point.

Ask probing questions, either as a reader or with colleagues, and use the case as it is meant—for thoughtful discussion of a district's strengths, areas for improvement, and more than as a comparison with your own or an ideal, as a launching point for discussing how the standard for professional learning strengthens educators' core work and makes possible greater student achievement. When you have delved deeply into the standard itself, the next step is to look within your own district to determine how the standard can be used to improve your system.

At the end of the case study, you will find a set of discussion questions to prime your reflection, analysis, and discussion. We encourage you to meet and discuss this district's use of data with a few colleagues and share your insights with other school and district staff.

W hat kind of data does the Aldine (Texas) Independent School District collect on each of the 64,000 students in the system? Raymond Stubblefield just laughs.

"Really, anything you want to know about a child," the Stephens Elementary School principal said. "We work hard at making sure we're looking at the high leverage points that affect student learning and making sure we have multiple sources of data."

These include traditional information: progress reports, grades, and state assessment results, including a statewide reading inventory given three times a year and state language acquisition tests. The school has a chart for each student with longitudinal data, such as whether the student has ever been retained, school history, and preK attendance. In addition, the school data sheet includes teachers' running records of the child's fluency, comprehension and campus formative assessment information updated every three weeks, and districtwide common assessments from every subject benchmarked every 18 weeks. Teachers have additional progress information from student portfolios and writing folders.

In a test-barraged culture, Aldine stands out as a district that has continually adjusted how and what student data it uses. More importantly, as Priscilla Ridgway, assistant superintendent of curriculum and instruction, points out drily, "We don't just collect the data. We do actually look at it."

Aldine ISD uses what it sees to constantly adjust—to plan what teachers need to know to better instruct students and to offer additional support where schools are lagging.

A New Beginning

Superintendent Wanda Bamberg recalls the late 1990s, when Aldine did not have the reputation for quality it now has. Student proficiency was low. Bamberg was in charge of curriculum and instruction at that time. In a meeting with the superintendent and deputy superintendent, the three reviewed what information they would need in order to use a scorecard based on the Baldrige quality framework.

"I'm looking at all this and I remember leaning over to (then-deputy superintendent) Nadine (Kujawa) and saying, 'This looks like a *whole* lot of work,' and she said, 'It *does*,'" Bamberg said. "But once we started it and started looking at goals and targets and asking questions, we realized it made a difference in what we were able to do as a district.

"You realize you perform better as a system because you're constantly looking at things that will make you say either, 'Hey, this is good; it's working,' or 'What are we going to do now? This is not going very well.' And if you wait until the year's over to look, it'll all come back and bite you."

Aldine's proactive approach to using data has resulted in steadily improving student achievement for a decade—with a student population that is mostly poor, highly mobile, nearly all students of color, and includes a large number of English language learners. Those characteristics, though, don't define the way the district sees "our kids," the phrase the educators there consistently used.

Aldine Independent School District is located in an unincorporated Harris County, Texas, just north of Houston. The district has 5 high schools, 5 ninth-grade schools, 10 middle schools, 11 intermediate schools, 33 elementary schools, 8 early childhood/preK schools, and a prekindergarten campus. Total enrollment is about 67,500 students, with 86% eligible for free or reduced-price meals. A handful of students speak one of five languages other than English, and an additional 31% are Spanish-speaking English language learners. Its student population is 2% white, 1% Asian/Pacific Islander, 70% Hispanic, 26% African American, and 1% other.

"The first thing I have to say is, our students are quite capable of learning," Ridgway said about her district.

Indeed, students' achievement has been acknowledged repeatedly at the state and national levels. Aldine won the Broad Prize for Urban Education in 2009, chosen from among the 100 largest urban districts in the country, for demonstrating "the greatest overall performance and improvement in student achievement while reducing achievement gaps among low-income students and students of color" according to the organization website (www.broadprize.org). The district had been a finalist for the prize three times before—in 2004, 2005, and 2008.

Broad selected the district because students exceeded the level of achievement predicted based on their socioeconomic status, and African American and Hispanic students narrowed the performance gap with white students in reading and in math at the elementary and middle grades. The district outperformed other Texas districts with similar demographics in 2007 in both reading and math at all grade levels.

The Texas Education Agency (TEA), the state agency responsible for public education, featured the district for its "collaborative monitoring and intervention" in the state's Best Practices Clearinghouse, reporting that the achievement levels of the district's at-risk, limited English proficient, and economically disadvantaged students on the state standardized exam were statistically significant compared with similar students in peer districts (TEA, n.d.).

These recognitions are the result of a clearly articulated curriculum aligned with state standards that is continually monitored at all

Figure 3.1   Aldine ISD Grades 3–11 TAKS Scores (Percentage
                  Proficient and Above)

School Year	Reading	Writing	Math	Social Studies	Science
2006–07	88%	94%	78%	91%	67%
2007–08	90%	93%	81%	93%	69%
2008–09	90%	93%	83%	95%	76%
2009–10	90%	94%	86%	97%	84%
2010–11	87%	90%	85%	96%	81%

Note: Texas switched its state assessment in 2011–12 to STAAR, a more challenging standardized exam that resulted in fewer students across the state reaching levels considered acceptable by the state. In 2013, 71% of all students in the Aldine district achieved at phase-in 1 Level II or above (satisfactory) on STAAR, an increase from 66% in 2012.

levels, from teacher to principal to area superintendents and central office administrators. When data show students aren't meeting expectations, the system kicks in with professional development for teachers to improve those weak areas. The data don't drive the district's success, but the information is the reason educators are able to continually improve, the superintendent said.

"Using data has helped us catch students (who are not succeeding) faster and earlier, and it's helped us be able to monitor our instruction better," Bamberg said.

CLEAR EXPECTATIONS FOR STUDENT ACHIEVEMENT

The change in the system began with an emphasis on curriculum, Bamberg said. District leaders formed teams of teachers to develop a common, districtwide curriculum. Teachers studied state expectations at every grade level in all content areas to create a set of grade-level expectations. They also met in vertical teams so each grade continued to build student knowledge, and the district created pacing guides so teachers would address the same skills at the same time during the year.

"We recognized that we have kids who move around, sometimes four or five times a year," Bamberg said. "If one school was following one scope and sequence and another school was following another scope and sequence, even kids moving within our own district would have gaps in what they were learning."

While the pacing is nonnegotiable, teachers have leeway in how they present the lesson. They all need to teach the targeted skills using district-approved materials, but how they work with the materials and how they meet the needs of their own students is up to them.

"We don't script the teachers," Ridgway said. "What is taught is spelled out, and we use a lot of the strategies that are best practices and research-based strategies across the district. But my chocolate cake might be a different recipe from your chocolate cake. It'll still be a chocolate cake. We don't take away the teacher's creativity or tell them every word to say and how to say it. That's why they're teachers."

ALIGNING THE CURRICULUM, ASSESSMENTS, STANDARDS

Once the district had curriculum guides in place for every subject K–12 and aligned with state standards, teachers had several years to work with the new expectations and develop lessons. Then they were back to work again on a new challenge—common districtwide assessments. Teams developed the assessments based on the outlined grade and subject expectations. Teachers also collaborated by subject and grade level at some schools to develop campuswide tests to augment the districtwide assessments.

Early on, Bamberg said, testing was more frequent and depended on how students performed. When the district found a weak area, for example, students would be monitored every few weeks to determine whether teachers were keeping on top of the planned curriculum.

"Until you get your curriculum out there and everybody is following it, assessments are no good," Bamberg said. "We have to ensure that every child is getting access to what's supposed to be taught at that grade level. Then we have to be sure it's assessed appropriately.

"When we first started giving the districtwide tests, the teachers would complain and say, 'That's a bad item,'" she continued. "From time to time we did have a bad item, and we'd throw it out.

But what more often happened is we discovered the teacher wasn't teaching that concept to the level of difficulty we were testing it on. We were following the state expectations for that concept, so it was truly a matter of our instruction not being aligned with what was written in the curriculum and what we were testing. That has helped us focus on improving instruction, and we use the data to improve instruction.

"It also helped us use the data to keep up with students and not wait until they got an *F* on their report cards to intervene and give them some assistance."

MONITORING THROUGHOUT THE SYSTEM

To keep track of all the data, the district purchased eduphoria!, an online application that can be used to track teacher appraisals, professional development, facilities usage, lesson planning, and student achievement data. A second system tracks additional student information, such as discipline and attendance.

Through eduphoria!, educators have nearly instant access to student assessment results and can have the data disaggregated and results color-coded. The idea is that a teacher can give a class a test, walk the answer sheets down to a scanner, and by the time the teacher returns to the classroom, have the assessment results waiting online. The teacher then knows how many students missed any one question; how students performed by gender, socioeconomic status, race, and ethnicity; and can have results broken down by students receiving program services such as ELL or special education. The information allows the teacher to immediately address concerns and reteach content to students who need reinforcement.

"We wanted that teacher to be able to look at that data and be able to make changes in classroom instruction the very next day," Bamberg said.

In addition to classroom teachers reviewing the data, principals are responsible for monitoring student progress in order to support teachers and students. Principals in each feeder system within the district meet every six weeks with an area superintendent to review the data from their schools. They look at grade-level and subject results. The district's curriculum directors monitor the data and pass reports to the superintendent's cabinet, comprising assistant superintendents and area superintendents. Bamberg looks at districtwide results two to four times a year in meetings with the area superintendents. She also checks informally in visits to schools.

"A really good principal is able to tell me which group is struggling and what they are doing to address that issue," Bamberg said. "They know who's struggling because they're looking at their data weekly or biweekly, whereas I'm not looking at that until it's been a grading period or a benchmark assessment. The most important pieces of the data are going to reside on our scorecard, and that's taken to the board, and then pieces of the scorecard wind up on my evaluation."

The superintendent also meets with principals in the summer to review their results. She asks the principals of schools with standout scores in an area, such as middle school math or high school biology, to present to the group information about how they achieved that result.

"A lot of times," Bamberg said, "it's a matter of letting the schools know that this is important and we're looking at this data— that keeps it on their radar. One of the things that central office does is to support and remind people, and we always make sure the system's in place so a school can look at the data easily."

SUPPORT FOR STUDENT LEARNING

Bamberg said that to reach that point, district leaders needed to change the culture so everyone understood the raised expectations and also needed to align teachers' professional learning with student improvement goals.

"One of the things we had to work through the culture to do was to create the expectation that there is going to be a common planning meeting, and it's a data meeting," Bamberg said. "Teachers had to get used to the idea that, 'We're going to come with our results, you're each going to have your results, and we're going to talk about what the kids did well on and what they did poorly on.'"

Teachers identify areas of student need, and then they work to develop the skills they need to address those specific areas. The district support includes staff at all levels working continuously on learning ways to improve instruction.

"Using data has changed professional learning in that we try to tie learning back to a specific issue," Bamberg said. "I remember when we would go through a needs assessment where teachers would give us all these topics they wanted to learn about. We don't do that anymore. We use the data to determine what the topics are. A teacher might say, 'I want some more professional development on manipulatives,' but we're going to use the data to tie our professional development more specifically to the concepts and the overall strategies that are good for math."

Several systemwide strategies for professional learning are in place.

Common Planning Time. District leaders encourage principals to schedule time for teacher collaboration during the day. Teachers also frequently meet on their own time after school. Secondary schools generally are able to schedule common meeting time, as do some elementary schools. As teachers review their data and plan lessons together, they share strategies.

Districtwide Learning. District staff review state assessment data each summer to make curricular and professional development decisions. The district focuses on common goals, such as developing professional learning communities or a writing strategy, and provides districtwide professional learning. Educators are required to engage in 40 hours a year of formal professional development.

Educators have options to complete some district learning opportunities online. They can take a course and print a certificate at completion. The district also can evaluate the online professional development through tests of the content at the end of the course in addition to a brief survey of the attendee's response to the course effectiveness.

An intranet database allows teachers to access model lessons colleagues have created and the district's curriculum directors have screened for quality. "We need to make sure people understand what that standard said, what it looks like when you teach it, what products could look like," said Sara Ptomey, executive director of curriculum and instruction.

Curriculum Directors and Skill Specialists. The district restructured central office staff to create program director positions, three each for math and English, specializing in preK–4, 5–8, and 9–12. Two directors each cover science and social studies, divided preK–6 and 7–12. Curriculum directors also are in place for visual arts, performing arts, dyslexia, and library media services. Program directors are responsible for the curriculum and instructional materials. They review the benchmark assessments and provide professional development.

"In many districts, you'll find a professional development department, an assessment department, and a curriculum department," Ptomey said. "But they don't talk to each other. Our district thinks that's ridiculous," and so created the curriculum director positions.

Curriculum directors offer professional development during the workday, evenings, and over the summer. They offer sessions at a principal's request; coach in the school, such as demonstrating guided reading to teachers; or facilitate a teacher team during teachers' common planning period. They visit classrooms to observe teachers and provide guidance and feedback.

A primary focus, however, is to coach schools' assistant principals for curriculum, the principals, and school skill specialists. Every campus has at least one skill specialist, and most have a specialist in language arts and one in math. Many campuses allocate Title I money to additional support to have a specialist who may focus on certain grades, such as just primary, preK–2, and have another for third and fourth grades. Decisions are made at the school level.

Each nine weeks, curriculum directors meet for three hours with skill specialists in their content area for professional learning specific to what students will learn in the coming nine weeks.

To get everybody using the same language, Ptomey said the curriculum directors then meet for 45 minutes with assistant principals from the campuses in each content area, and with principals for a total of an hour, each director providing a 15-minute overview of what instruction should look like in the coming grading period.

District balanced literacy trainers and balanced numeracy trainers also provide school specialists with monthly professional development in those areas. The goal is that, with leadership support, the specialists offer professional development to teachers at their sites. Grade-level or department chairs or a school skill specialist lead teacher data meetings and help teachers focus on strands that may need to be retaught.

Each curriculum director also is responsible for five "accelerated" campuses, schools that are showing signs of falling behind academically. The directors spend time weekly on each campus to provide additional instructional support in identified areas of need.

"We do a lot of training of trainers because we're so large (that) it's difficult to pull teachers out during the day," Ridgway said. "We depend a lot on campus leaders to learn and go back and provide support."

Learning for School Leaders. School leaders meet with the curriculum directors additionally, in quarterly data meetings that also include area superintendents. They review common assessment data and decide next steps for curriculum and instruction. When these teams identify broader, districtwide strategies, Aldine makes sure that principals and assistant principals are trained first so they know what to look for to evaluate how teachers are implementing what they are learning, because the administrators "are the ones who are going to be walking in and out of the classrooms every day," Bamberg said. "You don't want your teachers to have more knowledge about an initiative than the people who are going to monitor their instruction."

TEACHER EVALUATION AND RECRUITMENT

District data don't pertain only to students. A new district teacher evaluation system, dubbed INVEST and developed with Charlotte Danielson and other consultants, was piloted for a year and then fully implemented beginning in 2013–2014. The system sets up structured conferences before and after principals observe teachers in their classrooms and encourages data-driven conversation based on evidence the principal collects.

Evaluations are tied to student growth in comparison with all district students. The objective is to have each student attain at least one year's growth. The intent is to provide teachers with information to use to improve their practice. Teachers can use the data to develop individual professional learning plans.

"We're looking at percentage of student growth," Ptomey said, "but more importantly, at professional responsibilities. INVEST looks at what the classroom instruction looks like. It considers the planning, so teachers are supposed to be in collaborative planning meetings. A professional learning community is not a time of day, it's a culture. INVEST is also going to help us make some decisions on how to help teachers move forward and what support they need."

System leaders also collect data on teacher morale, school climate, and teacher turnover, including how many retired, left the district, or moved, among other things. These data help improve the system's work, including targeted hiring. Teachers are actively recruited from across the country by staff who make contacts at national career fairs and connect with top teacher preparation programs.

A Culture of Data-Driven Decisions

Fourth-grade language arts teacher Brenna Dorgan arrived five years ago at Stephens Elementary School, far from her native Michigan, attracted by the quality of urban education Aldine ISD offers. As a student intern, Dorgan was frustrated by the education students in inner city Grand Rapids, Michigan, were receiving. At a career fair, she sat down with an Aldine human resources professional to find out how Aldine was doing with similar students and was recruited.

"Even for as old as our actual building is, we're surrounding our kids with literature in all subject areas," Dorgan said. "Work is posted everywhere. It's just a very warm, conducive environment for learning and I fell in love with it, walking around feeling all the learning that was happening."

The National Center for Urban School Transformation recognized Stephens as a National Excellence in Urban Education winner in 2010, and the school also has been a Title I Distinguished School for 10 consecutive years. It has received an "exemplary" rating from the Texas Education Agency, the state's education accountability system, for 12 years. These achievements have come from the work of approximately 1,000 students, 90% of whom are Hispanic and 8% African American (the remainder are white). Nearly 9 in 10 students are from economically disadvantaged families and more than half are English language learners. How did they achieve high levels of learning?

At Stephens Elementary, Dorgan said she and other teachers routinely use their planning time to observe each other, compare lessons, and reflect on which strategies are most effective with students. They routinely compare assessment results for students in their classes.

"With the relationships we've formed with one another, we've set aside individual sensitivity," Dorgan said. "We're constantly reminded that even though it's hard sometimes to expose yourself in that way as a teacher, really only good things can come out of it. We know it's for the greater good of our kids."

Teachers assess student writing samples from the children's writing portfolios every grading period and check math skills using common assessments every three weeks. Dorgan works each week during a common planning time with a dozen or so upper elementary language arts teachers in a meeting facilitated by a team leader. Skill specialists work with the teacher teams on strategies to support bilingual students, Response to Intervention, or creating common assessments. They look at each child's progress. Teams analyze student data and plan differentiated instruction, reflect together, conduct their own book studies, or follow up on schoolwide book studies.

At a recent whole school faculty meeting, teachers discussed and responded to a book the principal asked them to read for a schoolwide push to improve learning. Team leaders shared their progress from teacher team meetings.

Principal Raymond Stubblefield said having classroom teachers guide, support, and facilitate the learning teams is a powerful form of accountability as teachers take ownership of the improvement process. Although he reviews student tracking charts, the school's classroom teachers, lead teachers, and skill specialists all closely monitor student progress and take responsibility for intervening when any child is falling behind—with "guidance and support from the administrative team," Stubblefield noted.

"Even within my role as principal, for example, when I'm checking report cards I'm looking at a different set of data," Stubblefield said. "I make sure there's alignment and calibration between where a student is instructionally and how that aligns to their grades. When I'm working with my intervention teachers on which kids are moving in and out of Tier II and Tier III in Response to Intervention, I may be looking at a different tracking chart for a different purpose."

But what happens in the classroom with the data makes a difference. When students practice lessons, teachers pull small groups and work with them on targeted skills.

"Teachers differentiate their instruction based on the data," Kathryn Heinze, the school's instructional coach, said. "Grade-level team planning is a lot of data analysis and developing specific strategies based on that data analysis. We have a constant tab on where kids are, and if we can't memorize it, we have a chart."

Stephens initially assessed students every six weeks in all subjects, but that changed in 2013–2014. The pullback had begun even before the state issued new regulations after citizen complaints of too much testing. Now, Aldine students take the districtwide common assessments every 18 weeks in each subject. School common assessments and teacher formative assessments fill in the information gaps in between, with schoolwide assessments every three weeks.

"Because I'm saying we have lots of sources of data, that doesn't mean we're doing lots of assessment," Stubblefield said. "Some of the assessment pieces are informal. For example, if you're talking about a student record that is going to give me good accurate information about where a kid is in terms of their reading level, that's done in small groups and it takes just a few minutes. There are lots of assessments that don't take that long that are still really meaningful in terms of giving you a picture of where the kids are."

Stubblefield looks for trend data to determine what professional learning teachers need and ties that to additional summer professional development and consultants he brings in regularly with Title I money.

While the district looks closely at the impact of professional learning on student outcomes, it does not necessarily conduct formal evaluations of the learning.

"The ultimate thing you want to have happen is have student achievement increase, so that's really what you're looking at in terms of analyzing the data—are students continuing to increase in terms of academic achievement," Stubblefield said. "Has the professional learning had the intended outcome? It's not just about whether the teachers went to professional development and started a new strategy, although that has to be followed through, too, so you're using instructional rounds to observe whether it's being practiced.

"If you're talking about a new initiative, it's making sure the teachers understand that you're going to give them the training and support and resources they need to do it, but there's also going to be the accountability to themselves and the campus that it's going to be done."

Long-Term Commitment

Using data is a long-term commitment, Bamberg said.

Bamberg said district leaders again are evaluating their student evaluations, looking at every grade level and subject to identify which might need additional assessment. In addition, she said the district is moving to project-based student assessments that are more seamless within the course of teachers' instruction rather than the paper-and-pencil, multiple-choice versions.

"We're trying to do a mix of things that will help kids do a better job with the rigor and the writing," Bamberg said. "We had to look at what every kid is having to do, so we're trying to stagger a lot of the exams. Our testing schedule has gotten a lot of revision over the years."

Ptomey said the district has reviewed its needs and is working to continue to improve some fundamentals—the graduation rate and reading. The state instituted a new standardized exam with more rigor, and the district's achievement scores dipped.

"We know we really need additional support for teachers on teaching reading," Ptomey said. "Our scores mean 30% of our kids can't read at grade level. That's not good. Although there are people who would be very happy with that (given the student population), that's inexcusable. It's a horrible sense of urgency to make sure every kid can read at grade level."

This focus on monitoring each student's progress and constantly tweaking instruction is what keeps Aldine moving forward.

"It's just a part of our culture," Ridgway said. "It's what we *do*."

THE VIEW FROM THREE ROLES

WANDA BAMBERG, superintendent

Initially we had to set up the expectations. When we first started off, we were in an achievement crisis. And so our approach was very top-down. We did not come in with a group of people sitting around in a room sharing good feelings. We brought in a team that we wanted to come up with the answers, we got the answers, and we told people, "This is what we're going to do." We weren't necessarily harsh, but we said, "We will be giving these assessments."

We had to ensure all kids were getting the instruction they were supposed to have as the first step. We said, "We're all going to teach *this*," and outlined strategies. After one year, people saw what a difference it made for kids, and teachers were looking at their own data that showed our kids did so much better that year than they did the prior year. When they realized our kids really could do it, they were willing to do anything. Then we moved on to creating common assessments.

In the beginning, Nadine Kujawa, my predecessor as superintendent, did not require the schools to give us their data. She wanted to let people get used to giving the assessments first. The first time we got the data, everybody freaked. Some teachers, including some biology teachers, weren't following the scope and sequence we had outlined. They hadn't learned that the assessments would tell us that, and so their data were really bad.

District administrators met with a group of the biology teachers, and the teachers said, 'We didn't have time to teach the whole unit.' They were spending four weeks on genes and the unit was two-and-a-half weeks. So their children did not do well on the assessment. We didn't hold it against the children, but we made it clear to the teachers: "You have to teach this curriculum, and you let us know if there's a problem. If you just are teaching your 'love unit' on genes—who can roll their tongue, who's got blue eyes and brown eyes, interview family members—you're going to wind up not having enough time to teach your full unit, and your children are not going to benefit because they will not have complete instruction in what they were supposed to have."

We had to do some lessons with teachers. Once the teachers got the hang of it, they really saw that kids could benefit. Kids who had not done well in the past did better because we were holding teachers accountable for teaching the curriculum. Looking at the data cannot be separated from the idea of what it is you're supposed to be teaching.

Currently, our writing scores in fourth and seventh grades need improvement. As a district-level team, the district-level program directors looked at the data, decided what training is needed, and are finding out what support teachers need. Teachers are saying they're struggling with teaching expository because of changes in what kids are asked to do based on higher standards. So as a district, we have to

(Continued)

(Continued)

go back, look at our data, talk to people, and then make new plans for professional development.

❧

RAYMOND STUBBLEFIELD, Stephens Elementary School principal

Data are used throughout the building. We've worked really hard to make sure we're looking at the data that will give us the most insight into where a student is. Initially we were heavy on planning and preparation—on looking at what our teams did. We needed to develop a common understanding of how we plan around core elements. Now that's evolved.

Last year and especially this year for our teams, particularly in the third- and fourth-grade teams, we are using protocols to look at student work. We've always done data analysis in our teams, but now we are really being intentional about drilling down to student work and student thinking and student learning instead of just working on the planning and preparation side.

As a campus, we have collective targeted areas. Any decision that we make on our campus is always based on data. It's always based on student needs that we identify through data analysis. A few years ago our focus was primary writing, for example, based on what the data showed. The district is very supportive of additional professional development, and so at the campus level, we go out to find people that we need to bring in. All of this is covered with our Title I money that I can use at the campus level.

Before that, we were working particularly around fluency, and we had Timothy Rasinski from Kent State University come in, because he's probably the leading person in the country on fluency. We just established a partnership with Teachers College in New York to work with Lucy Calkins' reading/writing project. This summer, we had a weeklong institute on reading workshop to develop a more rigorous practice in reading instruction. All of our teachers went through the whole week of that, and we've had consultants come in during the year for follow-up. Also, we converted one of our Title I positions from being an intervention teacher to being an instructional coach to work directly with teachers.

We were very intentional as a school about working collaboratively in teams, so we made sure we have common planning periods in the schedule. Our district does not have early-release days, but we asked for a waiver six days a year to have an early-release day to give teachers another two-and-a-half hours together each time to plan collaboratively. Three times during the year I bring in substitute teachers to cover classes so teachers have entire half-days to plan. Teachers also often meet after school on their own time.

I'm always trying to model what I want for the teachers—and that's to be a learner. So I, too, constantly seek out the very best. I'm continually reading and working on my understanding around best practices. The other thing is being honest and open and reflective with the staff about things that I'm still learning. We have a saying on campus, that we are *all* here to learn. That has to start with myself, and then it trickles down to the teachers and the students.

BRENNA DORGAN, fourth-grade language arts teacher

Data analysis happens on so many different levels. There are district-wide benchmarks, there's STAAR state testing, the lower grades do TPRI, all the grades test fluency and comprehension levels with running records. Then as teachers, we look at ourselves in different realms—how are we compared to the district, how do we compare within our school, how do our student groups compare.

Third- and fourth-grade language arts teachers plan together, and within that team is where we do most of our data analysis. We keep one spreadsheet for each student where we're trying to see the kid's progress, benchmarks, report card grades, progress reports, comprehension levels, fluency. We're trying to make sure it all aligns and that we're being responsive to the students' needs when we're planning together, when we're planning in our own classrooms, and in the conversations that we're holding with students. It's all based on evidence and data. We're being proactive as well as reactive in our analysis.

We respond to the data in many different ways. One thing I try to do as much as possible is to be transparent with the students. So when I'm looking at data, I'll do some analysis, but I want the students hands-on and involved in the analysis as well. That's something over the years I've pushed harder for. The teacher shouldn't be the only one analyzing data

(Continued)

(Continued)

and reflecting. In my room, I call it complimenting ourselves on things and having a new focus for next time. The students have their own fluency and comprehension data that they monitor on their own. That's done in most third- and fourth-grade classrooms at some level. It really helps to be constantly involving the students with it.

Alignment is something we really focus on with all the data we have—identifying why a student is reading at this level but struggling on a test. That's a conversation our team just had: This student's comprehension level is this, but when they're reading a test and answering questions, they seem to be a little bit off. We're trying to figure out why. We have a high level of English as a second language and limited English proficiency students, and I have quite a few bilingual students for whom this is their first year of full English instruction, so a lot of them are struggling with a language barrier.

The biggest help to me is that data allow me to identify student strengths and weaknesses and to be responsive quickly in small groups, conferencing with individual students, and with class groups. And I have whole-group conversations in my classroom about what it really means to make a goal and to strive to change what we would like to change.

Note: Quoted material from Wanda Bamberg, Brenna Dorgan, Kathryn Heinze, Priscilla Ridgway, Sara Ptomey, and Raymond Stubblefield is used with permission.

CASE STUDY DISCUSSION QUESTIONS

1. How do educators in the Aldine district use the data they collect to affect teacher learning in ways that will improve student learning? How does your district use the data it collects?

2. What does the case study demonstrate about how data can be used in professional learning at the school level? At the system level?

3. What is the district's role in collecting data? What do you see in the case that is noteworthy about the district's role? What drawbacks are evident in the district's data collection? What do your district leaders do to use data to improve teacher and student learning?

4. Who should decide how much and what types of data to collect? How did Aldine make those choices? Who currently makes those determinations in your system?

5. What additional sources of data would help teachers, school leaders, and district administrators in your system make decisions about professional learning?

6. What evidence does Aldine use for how effective professional learning is for teachers? What evidence does your district have for the impact of professional learning? Where would you place your evidence on Thomas Guskey's levels?

REFERENCE

Texas Education Agency. (n.d.). Collaborative monitoring and intervention model—Aldine ISD. Retrieved from http://www.tea.state.tx.us/Best_Practice_Summaries/Collaborative_Monitoring_and_Intervention_Model—Aldine_ISD.aspx

Index

Accountability:
 attainment data, 22
 improvement data, 22
 large-scale assessment data, 3–4, 7,
  31–32
 value-added models, 22
Affective data:
 professional learning evaluation, 32
 student learning goals,
  7–8, 14–15, 32
Aldine Independent School District
 (Texas):
 academic proficiency scores
  (2006–2011), 82*f*
 case study discussion questions,
  96–97
 case study introduction, 78–79
 common planning time, 86
 curriculum directors, 86–88
 data-driven decision making, 89–91
 district demographics, 81
 districtwide assessments, 83–84
 districtwide learning opportunities, 86
 educational awards, 81–82, 89
 long-term commitment, 92
 multiple data sources, 79–80
 principal perspective, 94–95
 principal role, 84–85
 principal training, 88
 proactive approach, 80–82
 professional evaluation system,
  88–89
 professional learning strategies,
  86–88

professional recruitment data, 89
 progress monitoring system,
  84–85
 skill specialists, 87–88
 Stephens Elementary School,
  79–80
 student achievement expectations,
  82–83
 student learning support, 85–88
 superintendent perspective, 92–94
 superintendent role, 84–85
 superintendent training, 88
 teacher perspective, 95–96
Attainment data, 21–22
Australia, 13

Bamberg, Wanda, 80, 82–84, 85–86,
  92–94
Behavioral data:
 professional learning evaluation, 32
 student learning goals, 7–8
Benchmark assessment, 58–62
Black Box evaluation, 66
Broad Prize for Urban Education
  (2009), 81

Case study. *See* Aldine Independent
  School District (Texas)
Cause-Effect Diagram, 53–54
Central tendency measures, 10
Classroom assessment, 15–17
 assessment defined, 16
 data standard, xiv, 7
 decision-making provisions, 16–17

Classroom observation, 62
Cognitive data:
    content areas, 12–13
    professional learning evaluation, 32
    student learning goals, 12–13, 32
*Common Core State Standards
    Initiative,* 13
Common formative assessment:
    collaborative development of,
        17–18, 19
    data analysis, 18–20
    illustration, 19*f*
    professional learning evaluation, 32
    student learning goals, 7
Complex Instruction Observation
    Tool, 56–57
Constructed-response assessment, 5
Continuous data, 9
Correlations, 10
Criterion-referenced assessment, 5, 22

Danielson, Charlotte, 88
Data:
    attainment data, 21–22
    context-specific nature, 2
    defined, 2–3
    essential guiding questions, 2–3
    forms of, 9–11
    functions of, 11–12, 75–76
    goals of, 6–8
    improvement data, 21–22
    levels of, 15–21
    multiple sources of, 3–6
    professional learning evaluation,
        23–37
    research summary, 37
    student learning goals, 12–15
    transparency in collection, 8
    types of, 9–12
Data forms:
    qualitative data, 10–11
    quantitative data, 9–10
Data functions:
    formative data, 11
    professional learning evaluation,
        75–76
    summative data, 11–12

Data levels:
    classroom data, 15–17
    district data, 20–21
    jurisdiction data, 20–21
    national data, 21
    provincial data, 21
    school data, 17–20
    state data, 21
Data standard:
    classroom assessment, xiv
    defined, xi, xiii
    educator data analysis, xiv
    professional learning evaluation,
        xv–xvi
    school-level assessment, xiv–xv
    student data analysis, xiii–xiv
    system data analysis, xiv
Data summary statement:
    description of, 53
    example of, 54*f*
Data Walk, 52–53
Discrete data, 9
District data, 20–21
Dorgan, Brenna, 89, 95–96

Educator learning needs:
    collective responsibility, 57
    Complex Instruction Observation
        Tool, 56–57
    educator involvement, 57
    KASAB format, 56
    professional learning decisions,
        56–57
    reflective questions, 56
    SMART goal format, 56
Educator progress assessment:
    benchmark system, 58–62
    classroom observation, 62
    formative data, 57–58, 64
    Innovation Configuration (IC)
        map, 62
    instructional rounds, 62
    knowing-doing gap, 58
    monitoring systems, 62–64
    Practice Profile, 63
    professional learning decisions,
        57–64

30–60–90 monitoring chart, 60, 61*f*
   walk-throughs, 62
Eduphoria!, 84
Elementary and Secondary Education
   Act, Title I, 4
Essential guiding questions:
   importance of, 2–3, 11
   qualitative data, 11
   quantitative data, 11
Expert knowledge, 10

Fishbone Diagram, 53–54
5 Whys protocol, 54, 55*f*
Formative data:
   educator progress assessment,
      57–58, 64
   examples of, 11
   function of, 11
   See also Common formative
      assessment

Glass Box evaluation, 66
Go for the Green protocol, 54

Hall, Gene, 62
Heinze, Kathryn, 91
Hord, Shirley, 62

Improvement data, 21–22
Innovation Configuration (IC) map:
   educator progress assessment, 62
   professional learning evaluation
      plan, 68, 70
Instructional rounds, 62
Interviews, 10
INVEST evaluation system, 88–89

Japan, 13, 14
Jurisdiction data, 20–21

Kanter, Rosabeth Moss, 59
KASAB format, 56
Kentucky, 64
Knowing-doing gap, 58
Kujawa, Nadine, 80

Language arts, 13
Large-scale assessment data:
   accountability purpose, 3–4, 7

professional learning evaluation,
      31–32
   psychometric quality, 3–4, 6
   reliability, 4, 6
   validity, 3–4, 6, 7, 31–32
Larson, L. C., 13
Learning Forward, xi–xii, xiii, 1, 4,
   12, 37, 45, 47

Mathematics, 13
Miller, T. N., 13
Multiple data sources:
   professional learning decisions,
      46–47
   student learning assessment, 3–6
   student learning needs, 51

National Assessment of Educational
   Progress (NAEP), 3
National Center for Urban School
   Transformation, 89
National data, 21
National Excellence in Urban
   Education, 89
Needs assessment survey, 46
New Teacher Project, The, 44–45
No Child Left Behind Act (2002), 3, 22
Nominal data, 9
Norm-referenced assessment, 5

Observation, 10
Open-ended questionnaires, 10

Performance assessment, 5
Performance-event assessment, 5
Portfolio assessment, 5, 7, 32
Practice Profile:
   educator progress assessment, 63
   example of, 63*f*
Professional learning decisions:
   data summary statement, 53, 54*f*
   educator learning needs, 56–57
   educator progress assessment,
      57–64
   monitoring systems, 62–64, 74–75
   multiple data sources, 46–47
   needs assessment survey, 46
   professional learning evaluation,
      65–74

professional learning programs,
    49–50
professional/student learning model,
    47–49
progress benchmarks, 58–62
reflective questions, 45, 46
research summary, 74–76
root-cause protocols, 53–55
student learning needs, 51–55
teacher survey, 44–45
Professional learning evaluation:
    assessment areas, 26–27*f*
    assessment questions, 26–27*f*
    Black Box evaluation, 66
    data collection method, 26–27*f*
    data utilization, 26–27*f*
    evaluation defined, 24–25
    evaluation questions, xv–xvi
    external evaluation, xv
    Glass Box evaluation, 66
    internal evaluation, xv
    investigative evaluation, 25
    learning strategies improvement,
        71–72
    levels model, 25–37
    merit/worth evaluation, 25
    planning model, 66–71
    professional learning decisions,
        65–74
    reflective questions, 65–66
    research summary, 37
    sound evaluations, 23–24
    student learning teams, 71–72
    systematic evaluation, 24
    theory of change, 72–74
Professional learning evaluation
        levels, 25–37
    backward planning process, 34,
        35–37
    comparison groups, 33–34
    context-specific nature, 36
    evaluation reliability, 33
    evaluation validity, 33
    experimental method, 32–33
    improvement implications, 34
    knowledge/skills significance
        (level 4), 27*f*, 30–31, 34
    meaningful comparisons, 32–34
    model summary, 26–27*f*

organizational support/change
        (level 3), 26–27*f*, 29–30, 35
    participant learning (level 2), 26*f*,
        28–29, 36
    participant reaction (level 1), 25,
        26*f*, 28, 36
    quasi-experimental method, 32–33
    return on investment, 34
    student learning goals (level 5), 27*f*,
        31–34, 35, 37
Professional learning evaluation plan,
        66–71
    data analysis, 67*f*, 70
    data collection, 67*f*, 69
    data collection location, 67*f*, 70
    data sources, 67*f*, 69
    information/data needed, 67*f*, 69
    Innovation Configuration (IC) map,
        68, 70
    measurable objectives, 67*f*, 68–69
    model summary, 67*f*
    program goals, 67*f*, 68
    SMART goal format, 68–69
    timeline, 67*f*, 70
Provincial data, 21
Psychometric quality of assessment
        data, 3–4, 6
Psychomotor data:
    professional learning evaluation, 32
    student learning goals, 14–15, 32
Ptomey, Sara, 86, 87, 92

Qualitative data:
    analysis procedures, 10
    collection methods, 10–11
    data form, 10–11
    essential guiding questions, 11
    formative assessment, 11
Quantitative data:
    accuracy of, 10
    analysis procedures, 10
    continuous data, 9
    data form, 9–10
    direct measures, 9
    discrete data, 9
    essential guiding questions, 11
    formative assessment, 11
    indirect measures, 9–10
    nominal data, 9

Questionnaires, 10–11, 28
Quotations, 10

Reflection data, 10
Reliability of assessment data, 4, 6
Research and Development Center
    (Austin, Texas), 62
Ridgway, Priscilla, 80, 81, 88, 92

School data:
    common formative assessment,
        17–20
    data analysis, 18–20
Selected-response assessment, 5
Self-reports, 10
SMART goal format:
    educator learning needs, 56
    professional learning evaluation
        plan, 68–69
    student learning needs, 53
*Standards for Educational and
    Psychological Testing,* 4
Standards for Professional Learning
    (Learning Forward), xi–xii
    Data Standard, xi, xiii, 1, 37
    multiple data sources, 4
    professional learning decisions, 45
    professional/student learning model,
        47–49
    student learning goals, 12
STARR state assessment, 82
State data, 21
Statistical analysis, 10
Stubblefield, Raymond, 79, 90, 91,
    94–95
Student learning goals:
    affective data, 7–8, 14–15, 32

backward planning process,
    34, 35–37
cognitive data, 12–13, 32
data domains, 12–1512–15
domain relationships, 14–15
psychomotor data, 14–15, 32
Student learning needs:
    data analysis, 51
    data summary statement, 53, 54*f*
    Data Walk, 52–53
    professional learning decisions,
        51–55
    root-cause protocols, 53–55
    SMART goal format, 53
Student learning teams, 71–72
Student subgroup data, 8
Summative data, 11–12
Surveys, 10–11, 28

Teacher-developed assessment, 5
Texas Education Agency (TEA), 81, 89
Theory of change:
    activities of, 73
    model illustration, 73*f*
    professional learning evaluation,
        72–74
    underlying assumptions, 72
30–60–90 monitoring chart, 60, 61*f*
Title I Distinguished School, 89
Transparency in data collection, 8
21st Century Skills (Larson & Miller), 13

Validity of assessment data, 3–4, 6, 7
Variation measures, 10

Walk-throughs, 62
Washington, 52–53

CORWIN
A SAGE Company

The Corwin logo—a raven striding across an open book—represents the union of courage and learning. Corwin is committed to improving education for all learners by publishing books and other professional development resources for those serving the field of PreK–12 education. By providing practical, hands-on materials, Corwin continues to carry out the promise of its motto: **"Helping Educators Do Their Work Better."**

Advancing professional learning for student success

Learning Forward (formerly National Staff Development Council) is an international association of learning educators committed to one purpose in K–12 education: Every educator engages in effective professional learning every day so every student achieves.